The Municipal Bond Market: Fundamentals

The Municipal Bond Market: Fundamentals

A Handbook for Professionals

Wilson White

VANTAGE PRESS
New York

Also by Wilson White

The Municipal Bond Market: Basics
The Municipal Bond Investment Advisor

FIRST EDITION

Published by Vantage Press, Inc.
516 West 34th Street, New York, New York 10001

Manufactured in the United States of America
ISBN: 0-533-12792-0

Library of Congress Catalog Card Co.: 98-90398

0 9 8 7 6 5 4 3 2 1

To Gretchen

Contents

Preface

I have written this, my third book on bonds, to provide an understanding of the fundamentals of municipals. I hope it will serve to lead the reader to the more complex levels of tax-exempts.

I've spent my entire professional life in this wonderful part of Wall Street. I worked for my father, Wilson (Pete) White, Jr., on his trading desk, way back in the 1940s. From 1954 through 1992 I was active in the business, especially the trading end, and ran my own firm for many years. I remain a registered rep and NASD principal, and serve as a consulting expert witness in tax-exempt cases. After spending most of my life in Summit, New Jersey, I now live in New York City.

I wish to acknowledge the substantial help and guidance of many fine people in researching and preparing this work, including: David E. Robbins and Pamela Golinski, Esqs., both of Kaufmann, Feiner, Yamin, Gildin & Robbins, New York; John Martin, DTC; Helen Kehrt, Jacksonville Electric Authority; Margaret Trapp, Bloomberg; Glenn Wright, Reuters; Chris McGuigan, J.J. Kenny; Joe Cinsale, S&P/Kenny; Frank Rizzo and Byron Klapper, Fitch; Jim Lebenthal, Lebenthal & Co.; Richard G. McDermott, Jr.; David Elliott and Greg Diamond, MBIA; David Goldstein and Hy Grossman, Standard & Poor's; George Leung, Moody's; Bill Jester and John Feery, PaineWebber; Joe Mysak, Grant's; Peter Hoey, FSA; Victor Liguori, Jay Peak; and last, but not least, Kit Taylor, MSRB.

Introduction: An Overview of the Municipal Bond Market

Have you heard the old story about how one blind man touches just the tail of an elephant, another just a leg, and a third its trunk and they all describe a very different animal? Well, we in municipals are luckier, because we can observe our subject as a whole. I see the municipal bond market in seven divisions: *the issuers,* or the communities that borrow by floating bonds; *the bonds* themselves; *the two marketplaces* where these bonds are bought and sold; *the services; the investors,* who put up the money to make it all happen; and, finally, our *regulators.* Now let's examine this wonderful beast, section by section.

The Issuers

Each public governmental unit, from states to sizable regional districts, such as Metropolitan Atlanta Rapid Transit Authority (MARTAS, we call their bonds), down to tiny places like Bloomfield Center Fire District, Connecticut, provides its citizens with needed facilities and services. The officials of these bodies, mostly elected, set policy for their professional staffs, oversee their work, face and respond to public opinion, and plan future goals. In addition, local governing bodies run their own financial affairs. Like most organizations, our communities pay this year's operating costs from this year's income. However, when a substantial long-term improvement, such as a new high school, is needed, communities usually borrow the money to build it. Enter municipal bonds, which provide them with cash to build now, and which are gradually retired from future income. Where does this income come from? From taxes, on real estate and income, and from other charges and fees and also from payments from state and federal governments. Bonds issued to benefit a community as a whole, primarily backed by real estate taxes, we call *general obligation bonds.* Bonds issued to build a facility which benefits some of a community's citizens, who pay according to their use of it, we call *revenue bonds.*

How do bond issues begin? Some places hold referendums, where voters have the final say. But elected public officials usually decide when public projects are to be built and when and how to finance them. In open and committee meetings and in executive sessions they debate and make many decisions, finally authorizing a new bond issue. Together state and local government units have been selling some $150 billion of new bonds per year, bringing the total outstanding in 1999 to about $1.25 trillion.

The Bonds

Principal

The U.S. Treasury, many larger corporations, and most of our municipalities borrow relatively large amounts of money by issuing bonds. What exactly is a bond? It's a kind of IOU or loan. Officially called a *debt instrument,* a bond is the legal evidence that a certain amount of money is owed.

This money to be repaid is called a bond's *principal,* or *face amount.* For instance, to improve its road system, Illinois may borrow $100 million by selling that many bonds. These are split into investor-sized units, typically of $5,000 each. The issuer borrows what it requires, and the bond buyers take just the amount they need. So Illinois uses the money to build roads and pays it back gradually, so much a year. And the investors get their principal back when it comes due.

Interest

Naturally, it costs money to borrow, and so, along with principal repayments, borrowers pay interest, giving investors a return on their cash. Interest is priced at such and such an *annual percentage rate* (APR). And "priced" gives us the right idea, because the price of borrowing money is its interest rate. If you take out a $100,000 mortgage at an interest rate of 7 percent, you will repay the lender $7,000 a year for renting the money, with principal payments extra. And when an investor lends to Illinois by buying bonds, it's the other way around. One hundred thousand dollars' worth of 5 percent bonds will return $5,000 every year until they are repaid.

Tax Exemption

Speaking of interest, most people think of municipal bonds as tax-exempt. And that is correct, in general. The federal government does not tax the interest on most municipals. Also, most states do not tax the interest on bonds issued within their own state. So a San Diego resident who owns Los Angeles County bonds pays no tax to either the IRS or California. We'll go into the reasoning and the exceptions later, but it's a fact—municipals are one of our few tax havens.

The Two Marketplaces

With all these bonds outstanding and more coming every year, it's not surprising that a market for municipals has developed. What is the purpose of this market? From the issuers' point of view, to borrow money at the lowest possible interest cost. But investors see it differently—they would like high returns. The job of the market makers—that is, the municipal bond dealers—is to help strike a price where both sides do as well as possible. When they are successful, they make a profit, usually less than one percent of principal.

The Primary Market

When homeowners need mortgage money, they go to a bank or other financial company. Similarly, when communities need construction money, they go to specialized securities dealers, called *underwriters,* who buy new issues from communities, and distribute them to investors. Underwriters stand between the community borrowers and the investor lenders, the three forming the complete primary market.

These underwriters usually form *syndicates*—that is, groups of dealers who buy an entire new issue and offer it in smaller lots. Let's say that a syndicate led by dealer PD buys the $100 million Illinois issue at a certain price. At that point it owns the bonds and is at risk. The syndicate then sets a single list of prices at which investors are offered the bonds. If the syndicate sells them as expected, then it will show a profit. However, should the syndicate fail to resell the bonds as planned, then it may show a loss.

The Secondary Market

After a new issue has been distributed, its bonds leave the primary and enter the *secondary,* or *trading,* market. There, instead of bonds being offered at one set price, their prices rise and fall freely, according to supply and demand. So if an investor who bought bonds in the primary market later wishes to sell the bonds, the secondary provides a market where traders compete against one another to pay the best price. Who are these traders? The approximately two thousand people employed by municipal bond dealers to help buy and sell tax-exempts for their customers. They sit on specialized desks, as we will see in Part Four.

The Services

A large number of companies provide services to the many municipal bond market participants. Three companies research new bond issues and rank them according to investment strength. Four substantial corporations insure issues against default. Some twenty specialized trading firms, the *brokers,* act as middlemen, buying from one dealer and selling to another, making a riskless commission in between. About fifty major law firms compete to provide legal services to issuers and dealers. And perhaps one hundred firms conduct a financial advising business, assisting communities to sell bonds advantageously. We will return to service providers in Part Five.

The Investors

Who owns all the billions of bonds? Of course, individual people. Who else owns anything? However, we classify them according to their holders: individuals directly and in tax-exempt packages, banks, insurance companies, and others.

Individual Investors

Many individuals buy tax-exempts directly. In fact, about one-third of all municipals are now owned by people in their own name or in their brokerage house accounts. They tend to own longer term bonds and to hold them until they are repaid.

The Bond Packages

There are two distinct types of municipal bond packages—unit trusts and managed funds. Together they are now by far the largest municipal buyers. Their sponsors create frameworks to buy, hold, and (sometimes) trade immense quantities of tax-exempts. Individuals buy pieces of trusts or funds, thus indirectly owning a proportionate share of their bonds and also receiving the same percentage of the interest. The package managers provide professional bond selection and monitoring, often charging a fee of about 1% of principal per year. In 1998 about half of all new issues went into the various packages.

The Banks and Insurance Companies

In 1998 commercial banks, who are subject to corporate taxes, were buying about 5% of new municipals for their own portfolios. However, special IRS regulations make owning larger quantities unfavorable to them. In addition, bank trust departments buy substantial numbers of tax-exempts for their fee-paying customers. Most property and casualty companies are stockholder-owned, taxable corporations, and when they are profitable, these companies often buy about 10% of all new issue municipals. The remaining municipals are bought and held by intermediate financial institutions, investment advisers, and also by dealers.

The Regulators

Like most industries, the municipal bond market operates under governmental supervision. In Part Seven we discuss our regulators—the SEC, the NASD, and the MSRB.

The Municipal Bond Market: Fundamentals

Part One

The Issuers

1

Forms of Government

Although Washington gets most of the headlines, the fifty thousand or so state and local community bodies do more of the actual governmental work. Stemming from earlier forms of democracy, such as town meetings, local governing bodies used to take simple, representative forms. Among their many duties, they issued their own bonds and repaid them from local sources of income. However, as citizen needs have grown more demanding and more complex, other bond-issuing governmental bodies have been invented. I fit them in four categories: the original representative bodies, regional districts, single-facility authorities, and conduit agencies.

Representative Bodies

Voters elect representatives to dozens of forms of local political entities, among them city and town councils, county commissions, and state legislatures. Most stay principally focused on their own local affairs. For instance, a city like New Paltz, New York, is governed by a town council, which draws up budgets and levies and collects taxes, among many other functions. Also, from time to time council members vote to borrow money by issuing bonds for public facilities, such as court and police buildings, water and sewer lines, and so on, serving the needs of its electorate.

In addition, some municipalities have expanded their interest boundaries. They have formed wider-based but still essentially local entities, including districts of many kinds. These include community college and hospital districts, irrigation districts, and even mosquito abatement districts, each governed by its own set of officials. For example, New Paltz and several other nearby Ulster County communities joined to create New Paltz Central School District, whose voters elect its board members. This district operates a substantial secondary school system that none of the underlying municipalities could have afforded alone.

Year after year the board oversees all the things necessary to run the system efficiently. It may see that one of its school buildings has become inadequate, and the community may face a decision to either renovate or replace it. In public hearings and private conversations, district board members listen and respond to public opinion about the problem. And then they may decide to go ahead and solve it. If it were a matter of buying a few computers or repairing a roof, districts often have enough cash. However, more substantial capital improvements are usually funded through a new bond issue. After deciding how much to borrow and how to repay it, the municipality sends the bond issue on to its marketing stage. We follow this process in the next chapter, where we'll see how financial experts go to work.

Regional Districts

Besides the localized political bodies, many communities facing a mutual need—water supply, sewage treatment, transportation, etc.—combine to form a large, regional entity to deal with it. The Lamar County Water Supply District, Texas; the substantial King County Metropolitan Sewer District, including Seattle, Washington; and the San Francisco Bay Area Rapid Transit District all serve citizens in many underlying governmental bodies. They may operate several facilities, augmenting them as the need arises.

The people who run such regional units are usually appointed by the elected officials in the participating communities. Their staffs often include specifically trained and highly qualified professionals. The boards of these entities must refer to the political area for guidance but authorize their directors and other personnel to make the day-to-day decisions. For instance,

New York and New Jersey may authorize their Port Authority to sell certain types of bonds, but its finance people set the exact amounts and the timing.

Most such issuers provide service to their users in varying amounts and charge according to use. So anyone who uses the Holland or Lincoln Tunnel, the George Washington Bridge, or a New York airport pays for the privilege. These streams of income cover the toll collectors' salaries, the general administrative expenses, and the interest and principal on the Port Authority's almost $5 billion bonds.

Single-Facility Authorities

Many public facilities serve a highly specific need of some of its citizens. To serve these needs, most states have created independent government entities to build and operate one project. Some recreation facilities, many hospitals, and most convention centers are financed through such project financing. The names Frank G. Bonelli Park and Recreation Authority, Martin Luther King, Jr. South East Hospital Authority, and Los Angeles Convention and Exhibition Authority, all in Los Angeles County, identify their functions. Single-facility projects are also operated by professional, appointed staffs. Their bonding ability is determined by enabling state legislation, and they assess taxes or charge the fees from which bondholders are repaid. Approximately five thousand single-project authorities now serve their users and their bondholders.

Conduit Agencies

In addition, some bodies lend their name and tax-exempt privilege to either government units or private corporations in the public benefit. Unlike single-facility authorities, these conduit agencies are purely financial and do not get involved in the operations of the facility. They serve as channels between the income-producing projects and the investors who lent them the money to build these facilities. For instance, the Chesterfield County Industrial Development Authority, which has issued over $200 million of environmental control revenue bonds for Virginia Electric & Power Company, consists of a few people in a small county office. They definitely let VEPCO run the power plants.

Also, since the 1970s many agencies have similarly financed tax-exempt single- and multifamily housing, and also health facility projects, each serving a specific public need. In each of these a state or locality votes to initiate a program, sells bonds for it, and through a designated agency provides financing. The agency merely collects lease or mortgage payments to repay bondholders. About five thousand industrial, housing, and other conduit agencies are now in service.

In Later Years

Soon after most new issues have been distributed, they tend to recede in the eyes of Wall Street. However, the communities' work continues for as many years as their bonds stay outstanding. Budgets have to be drawn up annually, taxes and charges adjusted and collected, projects maintained, and interest and principal payments sent on time. And, increasingly, the community is obligated to provide a steady flow of financial information to bondholders and other interested parties. These documents include the audited yearly financial statements, records of bond sales and redemptions, and income and expense sheets.

During the early 1990s many municipalities kept their investors in the dark about significant financial strains. This led to loud calls for higher levels of municipal financial information. Our regulators have no jurisdiction over local issuers but soon figured out a way to require more *disclosure*. Now we can't underwrite a bond issue unless the community agrees to provide the specified information. More on disclosure in Chapter 4.

2

Designing a Bond Issue

After the pols have decided to borrow, they send bonding authorization to their trained financial people to implement. Many larger communities employ up to several dozen financial experts. They manage money, apply for grants, provide the bond market with current municipal information, and when necessary, create bond issues. Other communities turn to the private sector to hire *municipal finance consultants* to do this work. I have written about Clearwater, Florida, and Kenosha, Wisconsin, both of whom are happy to use outside consultants.[1] The goal of both is the same: to design a serviceable new issue at the lowest possible borrowing cost. How long between the time bonds are authorized and the time they are actually sold? Usually a minimum of one month, but often longer.

To comply with state enabling laws, conform to securities regulation, and satisfy investors, most municipal bond issues include certain basic features. Among these are a *legal opinion,* one or more service *ratings, credit enhancement,* and, officially describing these, a definitive *official statement.*

The Official Statement

The central document in any municipal new issue is the *Official Statement* (O.S.). One of the first items finance departments start to work on, it is supposed to provide all the information an investor needs to understand an issue. They also provide protection for both issuers and dealers from unwanted liability. O.S.s are assembled and written by the issuers, sometimes with substantial help from underwriters. The SEC mandates that each syndicate member, especially managers, thoroughly review an issue's preliminary O.S. before bidding on it. These are also distributed to potential buyers.

O.S.s contain: a full description of the issuer; the exact nature of the security backing the bonds offered; all pertinent features of the bonds; historical information about the source of payment; and a description of the issue's legality, including its tax status. After the sale, a final O.S. is printed, with all the definitive information—coupons, prices, ratings, and all the rest. With so many eyes on the O.S., you can see why finance people would start working on it as soon as an issue is announced.

The Legal Side

Another of the first issuing steps is getting the lawyers involved. Attorneys for issuers are called *bond counsel,* and their roles include verifying that an issue conforms to enabling laws, that it goes through any required validation procedures, and that the O.S. is correctly drawn. After these and other requirements are met, they write a *legal opinion* stating that the bonds have been properly issued in every respect, with what security, and exempted from or subject to which taxes. A copy of the legal opinion is printed on physically delivered bonds and included in the O.S. Lawyers for the dealers who buy the issue, the *underwriting counsel,* also review its legal status and guard the syndicate's interests.

The Ratings

Dealers and investors rely heavily on ratings to help determine an issue's interest rates and prices. Since rating a bond takes some time, finance people start sending out information early in the issuing process. Three major financial service companies: Moody's Investors Service, Standard & Poor's, and Fitch, research municipal bonds and rank them according to their credit strength. When the ratings are announced, the pricing can proceed. For more on ratings see Chapter 19.

Credit Enhancement

These days most bond issuers consider buying bond insurance or other credit enhancement in order to lower their borrowing costs. In fact, in 1998 over half of the new issue volume was insured. We return to credit enhancement in Part Five.

Notes

In addition to selling long term bonds, which may be likened to a family's taking out a home mortgage, communities often borrow temporarily by issuing various kinds of *notes*. Like credit card purchases, supposedly to smooth out irregular flows of income and expense. With one big difference—their interest rates are almost always lower than those on bonds. Note forms include *BANs* (bond anticipation notes), *TANs* (tax anticipation notes), among many others.

Note

1. Wilson White. *The Municipal Bond Market: Basics* (Jersey City: The Financial Press, 1985).

3

Floating a Bond Issue

Public or Private Sale?

Somewhere during the design process, finance people make a basic decision—how the bonds will be marketed. One choice is through public, competitive bidding. The other is through private, negotiated sale. Most smaller, general obligation issues are sold via the more traditional avenue of public bidding, and indeed, many states require this method. However, the modern trend is toward negotiated sales, where just one group is hired to market an issue. Many revenue bonds and many large G.O. issues are now being sold that way.

I—VIA COMPETITIVE BIDDING

Rooted in a distrust of public officials and in the spirit of fair play, about 75% of all new issues, especially smaller G.O.'s, sell competitively. It's similar to a community's asking for bids to supply fuel oil or paint for city hall, except that bond bidders compete to supply money. Although anyone may enter a bid, in practice nearly all are submitted by bond dealers. In recent years the number of new issues (including the tiniest ones) sold this way has averaged almost two hundred per week. From the community's perspective, the competitive road has four chief milestones: shaping the bidding specs, announcing the sale, receiving and awarding bids, preparing the bonds for delivery and payment.

Shaping the Issue

As we saw, in constructing an issue, the local government unit passes a bonding ordinance setting the issue's backing, the number of repayment years, and the total amount to be borrowed. Then the finance experts shape it within these parameters to achieve the best terms, including the lowest achievable borrowing cost. They take the politicians' decision on maximum debt service, and subtract estimated interest amounts to produce a rough principal schedule. Referring to the enabling rules, they will then set the bidding specifications: the minimum dollar amount, the allowable coupons, the form of the bonds, where and how they will be delivered, and many other essentials. They then send these design elements to bond counsel for review.

Announcing the Sale

When counsel's tentative approval comes back, the finance people prepare to set the exact time and place where bids will be received. To announce the sale they usually advertise in a local newspaper and in our trade journal, *The Bond Buyer,* which may print the "Official Notice of Sale" as a paid display ad. It and other municipal media then flash the news around the municipal market. Soon thereafter Wall Street takes its first steps to address the issue, with managers forming syndicates to bid on it.

Receiving the Bids

At the specified site and time, underwriting groups submit their bids, and the community officials, with the finance people at their side, open them to determine the winner. Often the bids come in as averaged rates called *true interest cost,* such as 5.77%, 5.66%, 5.70%, 5.68%, and 5.74%, where best is lowest, here the 5.66% bidder. Then the officials huddle to decide whether to accept the winning proposal. Once in a long while they reject all bids, but over 98% of the time they vote to award the bonds.

Preparing the Bonds

While the underwriting group goes to work to sell the issue, the community prepares the bonds for delivery. Here the lawyers come into action again, making sure that all the *i*s are dotted and the *t*s crossed, to ensure that both issuers and bondholders get their money's worth. In the old days most bonds were printed up as fine-quality certificates and physically signed and delivered to the buyers. Now, following changes in federal regulations, most are delivered in *book entry* form, whereby principal is recorded electronically, and interest sent out automatically. After two or three weeks the issue should be ready and a definite delivery date set. Then, at a bank or clearing house, the bonds are transferred to the underwriters, who pay the issuer the bid amount, as securities and money change hands. The group then redelivers the bonds to their customers, we may hope making a profit.

II—VIA NEGOTIATED SALE

Partly reacting to issuance abuse in the distant past, until the 1980s most states prohibited or tightly controlled negotiated sales. Until then, the few deals that were negotiated came from issuers such as the Indiana Turnpike Authority, where the uncertain prospects of a large unbuilt project made competitive bidding impractical. In such cases the issue had to be custom-designed, a syndicate group lined up, and skeptical investors convinced, a process requiring substantial interaction among issuer, lawyers, underwriters, and buyers. However, things have changed. Now communities have more freedom, and negotiated deals come out almost every business day. Although most small deals sell competitively, in 1998 about 80% of the total new issue volume, both revenue and general obligation, came out via negotiated sale. From the issuers' viewpoint the five chief negotiated mileposts are: choosing the managing underwriter, signing the negotiating contract, dealing with the manager as the issue develops, bargaining for final interest rates and profit margins, and awarding the bonds.

Choosing the Manager

Dealers compete with each other aggressively to be named managers of negotiated deals, offering the issuers ever more advantages and lower and lower costs. In fact, at the manager selecting level most negotiated deals are now at least as competitive as are publicly bid ones, so that in 1998 the top ten managers underwrote about 65% of all negotiated deals. Indeed, the community officials must get pretty confused at times, what with all the grand promises, but it seems that they are benefiting from the Wall Street rivalry. Underwriting spreads have nosedived almost 50%, from over $12 per bond ten years ago to under $7 now.

The Contract

After issuers choose a manager, both sides pledge cooperation, so that the deal can be successfully placed. Although some understandings are reduced to writing, few such contracts guarantee anything very specific, except that the parties proceed with good faith. Most underwriting fees are usually paid from the proceeds of the issue. No deal, no paycheck.

Dealing with the Manager

The issuer's finance department often proceeds much as they do in a competitive sale, but cooperating with the manager to produce the necessary documents—the legal opinions, the rating information, the O.S., and so on. Seasoned revenue issues, such as the well-known bonds of Tacoma's Light and Power Division or Austin's Utility Department, may present only a few problems to solve. These include the updating of income and expense figures for this and competing utilities.

On the other hand, when a brand-new agency tries to float an issue, managers more often take a leading role in designing it. During this process the managers keep a sharp eye on the bond market, the raters and insurers, and the needs of potential investors. The idea is to construct an issue that appeals to buyers so well that it produces the lowest total cost to the issuer and also returns the underwriter a worthwhile profit. This involves a great deal of consultation. For instance, in 1996 California's Foothill/Eastern Transportation Corridor issue had taken over a year to design and shape before talks with potential investors could even begin. We return to negotiated underwriting from the dealers' point of view in Part Three, "The Primary Market."

Bargaining

When a negotiated issue is ready to market, the issuer and the manager begin to bargain over additional security features, call provisions, expense levels, timing, etc. While the manager sets preliminary prices, the issuer may scrutinize underwriter relationships, advertising matters, allotment procedures, and, of course, interest rates and profit margins. Naturally, each side differs in its goals, but usually they reach the necessary compromises.

The Award

After the final pricing, as orders for the issue begin to flow in satisfactorily, but typically before the bonds are all sold, the issuer awards the bonds to the underwriting group. The attorneys for both sides agree on a document whereby the bonds are definitely sold by the community and bought by the syndicate. When the word goes out, "We've got the award!," investor interest usually peaks, and trading in the issue may soon begin. Then the syndicate and the issuer part, like the first and second stages of a rocket launch. The underwriters zoom on, carrying their risk, aiming for a profit orbit, while the municipality drops away from the marketing scene.

After the award is made, the syndicate process continues much like that of a competitive deal. The underwriter distributes the bonds, and the issuer prepares them, so that at delivery date bonds and money change hands.

4

In Later Years

Soon after new issues, whether competitive or negotiated, have been distributed, they usually recede in the eyes of Wall Street. However, the communities' work on its bond issues continues for as many years as they are outstanding.

General Obligation Bonds

For a community, G.O. issues resemble a family's mortgage payments—they are firmly built into their budgets. Whether for a city or a household, paying this debt comes first and foremost, both to stay current and to avoid credit difficulties. As noted, general obligations are secured by the full faith and credit of the municipality, payable from all sources, definitely including the real estate tax. To meet this prime responsibility, communities draw up annual budgets, usually for several years in advance, calculating their income and estimating expenditures. One part of this process is to assess each piece of local property, levy a fixed percentage tax on it, and send bills to the owner. Along with other income, the yield from this tax goes into the general fund and eventually to the bonds' paying agent, to meet both principal and interest. In practice, other community expenditures may have to be postponed so that debt service can be met. Delinquencies set off alarm bells all around the financial world. Who sees to it that all goes smoothly? From year to year, the local government body. From day to day, its finance officers.

Revenue Bonds

Issuers of revenue bonds operate quite differently. If G.O.s are tended like mortgage payments, revs are managed much like private enterprises. Again, budgets playing a leading part in their finances and are planned years in advance. Some cities run these public enterprises from within their local government, some by separate divisions, while others such as Jacksonville, Florida's Electric Authority, are semi-independent agencies. These enterprises deliver their product, pay its expenses, bill customers according to use, and from the operating profit send debt service to their bondholders. Revenue issuers also draw up and follow capital budgets, plan to replace facilities as they wear out, and provide for future expansion and improvement. Fortunately for them, most municipal enterprises operate monopolistically. Indeed, many are subject to regulation by their state public utility commissions.

Since revenue bond issuers don't give the G.O.s, unconditional pledge, more precise constraints are imposed on them. Revenue bonds are usually issued under an *indenture,* which sets out the issuer's duties. Among these is a promise to maintain a system in good condition, to refrain from impairing its income-producing power, and to charge rates adequate to cover both expenses and debt service. Many indentures name a trustee, usually a local commercial bank, to implement the indenture. The issuer sends monthly and annual reports to the trustee, so that it can monitor the system and protect the bondholders. Finally, if the issuer does not perform as promised, or ever fails to pay debt service on time, trustees may invoke the indenture default provisions that cover such unlikely events.

Refunding

Within the capital budget one item comes up from time to time—refunding. Under certain circumstances, a bond issue can be retired prior to maturity and replaced with another more advantageous to the issuer. Sometimes a currently lower-interest-rate environment makes this possible. Or special conditions within the issuer may make refunding desirable. In either case, bonds may be called in as agreed in the indenture and the old holders paid off, usually at a small premium over principal amount. Or the bonds may be refunded ahead of their stated call date by escrowing U.S. Treasury obligations to secure all its debt service, thus *defeasing* the old refunded issue and clearing the way for refunding. In this process, local municipal finance experts are often guided by dealer managers in search of new business.

Disclosure

During the early 1990s, tax-exempt market participants became increasingly apprehensive about the scarcity of financial data coming from many municipalities. Too often, issuers were keeping their investors in the dark about financial matters. But regulators have no power over state or local governments. So effective January 1996, the SEC amended its Rule 15c2-12, prohibiting dealers from underwriting or recommending any municipal unless the community provides certain financial information and "event notices" as long as the bonds shall live. These include:

1. Annual reports, including audited financial statements.
2. Rating changes.
3. Bond calls and defeasances.
4. Indications of financial difficulty, including unscheduled invasions of reserve funds, and changes of or draws on credit enhancers.
5. Debt service defaults of principal or interest.
6. Changes in bondholder rights or tax-exempt status.

All of this information goes to either a trustee or to a Nationally Recognized Municipal Securities Information Repository (NRMSIR). Municipal media specialists watch new postings in the repositories and broadcast significant items, such as rating changes, refundings, or calls. All this adds up to a lot of work for communities, no doubt contributing to the more ethical aura of municipal dealings.

5

Taxes and Municipal Bonds

Federal Income Taxes

Bond buyers often refer to the prices and yields on U.S. Treasuries, because they are the ultimate fixed-income benchmark—highly liquid and, for dollar investors, principal risk-free. However, interest on U.S. bonds is federally taxable, substantially reducing their real, take-home yields to individuals. So although a Treasury may show a nominal 5.00% yield, it returns taxable investors less than that. How much less depends on their tax bracket. In 1998 joint filers up to $40,000 will be taxed at 15%, up to $97,000 at 28%, to $148,000 at 31%, and to $264,000 at 36%, with a top of 39.6%.

Figure 1 shows a typical maturity scale of U.S. and tax-exempt yields, and also the effect of a 31% tax bite. In this bracket, a U.S. Treasury due in one year and nominally yielding 5.00% returns only 3.45% (5.00% x (1.00 - 31, or 69%) = 3.45%). This 3.45% after-tax return becomes the yield for municipals of the same maturity to beat. For instance, if some high-quality municipals due in the same year were offered at a 3.75%, an investor might be tempted to buy them instead of the Treasuries. But not at a 3.25%. Why take a payoff lower than you can get on our safest bonds of all—U.S. Treasuries?

U.S. Treasury vs. Tax–exempt Yields				
Maturity	**U.S. Treas.**	**@31%**	**Tax-exempt Insured**	**Tax-exempt A Rated**
1 year	5.00%	3.45%	3.75%	4.00%
5	5.25	3.62	4.00	4.25
10	5.50	3.80	4.25	4.50
15	5.60	3.86	4.50	4.75
20	5.70	3.93	4.75	5.00
25	5.80	4.00	4.90	5.20
30	5.75	3.97	5.00	5.25

Figure 1

Taxable Equivalent

There is also another way of comparing returns, called *taxable equivalent yields.* Start with the tax-exempt yield, and divide by what percentage investors keep after paying their tax. At 31% an investor keeps 69 cents on the dollar. For this bracket, divide the tax-exempt yield by .69 to get what a taxable bond has to yield to equal that. At 3.75% this comes out to 5.43% (3.75/.69 = 5.43).

How do these rates affect a 15% bracket investor? During the middle 1990s it was pretty easy to find safe taxable returns in the 7.00% range, while a tax-exempt yield of 6.00% was about as high as good municipals were bringing. At a 15% rate, a 6.00% was only the same as a 7.05% taxable, so low-bracket investors weren't better off buying tax-exempts. When we come to the higher federal brackets, where you get to keep only 69%, or even 60%, things change. At the same tax-free 6.00%, the equivalent was a taxable 8.69%, or even 9.93%. In those years governments yielded at most a 7.00%, and higher taxable returns were found only in lower-grade investments, where the extra yield was achieved at considerable extra risk. This gets to the main point about investing in municipals. *Tax-free bonds usually provide the top-bracket individual fixed-income investor with the highest available spendable returns.* And the ads aimed at such investors often feature taxable-equivalent tables to drive home this message. Tax-free interest is *not* reported by brokers on their reports to the IRS, but taxpayers are supposed to list it on their 1040 income tax form, line 8b.

Deductions

Many personal deductions were curtailed by the Tax Reform Act of 1986. However, the deductibility of *real estate taxes* and *state and local income taxes,* an indirect federal subsidy for municipalities, remains in effect. This ties into our discussion of local government economics and also relates directly to municipal bond investing.

The Tax Exemption

Congress took a good look at the tax-exempt bomb shelter during 1986 but decided not to drop anything on it directly. However, the new law cut back on many abuses, limiting the tax-exemption to issues that serve a genuine *public purpose.* No already-issued bonds were retroactively subjected to tax. However, the exemption of future new issues to finance corporate enterprises and private nursing homes and apartment buildings was severely restricted or eliminated. In anticipation of the reforms to come, tens of billions of dollars' worth of municipals were hastily issued and sold in 1985 and '86, and new bond sales almost doubled their normal volume, many of them with questionable motives and purposes. New flotations soon returned to their long-term patterns of growth, and the market now rests on firmer ground.

Federal Taxes on Municipal Bonds

Although we often call municipal bonds tax-exempts, that term is not 100% accurate. The IRS collects taxes from owners of municipals in three ways: in certain exceptional cases on their *interest,* on *capital gains,* and at *estate* time.

AMT

Interest on bonds issued to finance authentic public purpose projects—traditional municipal improvements such as roads, colleges, and water facilities, is 100% federally tax-exempt. However, many dodges, such as bonds floated solely to earn arbitrage profits, are now denied tax-exemption, and rightly so. Between these two categories—clearly public purpose bonds and prohibited abuses—falls a gray area of bonds that are public in purpose but don't quite meet Congress's requirements. For instance, although most of the Pennsylvania Housing Finance Authority's revenue bonds qualify for full tax-exemption, some do not quite meet the full public-purpose requirements. But this authority goes right ahead and sells new issues of them anyway. Bonds such as these are subject to the *alternative minimum tax.* What is the AMT? A federal levy designed to tax people with high special deductions (such as from passive-activity farming or oil drilling losses). If you deduct amounts substantial enough of such preference items, including incentive stock option plans, then interest on AMT municipal bonds has been subject (as of 1999) to a 26% tax. If a customer is in this class, watch out that the AMT doesn't get her. However, since AMT bonds often yield about 20 basis points more than other comparable municipals, they can offer most buyers a tax-exempt bargain.

Taxable Municipals

In addition, a very few communities have decided, for one reason or another, to deliberately issue *taxable municipal bonds,* which fail entirely to meet the public purpose test. These bonds are sold mostly to institutions, and interest on them is not Federally exempt.

Capital Gains and True Yield

Profits registered when securities are sold, including profits on municipal bonds, are treated separately from ordinary income. As with stock buyers, municipal investors who sell bonds or let them mature at a profit may owe tax on the gain. The 1999 federal capital gains rate is 20%, and in addition, gains are often subject to state and local taxes. Sales or redemptions of all securities, municipal bonds included, are reported to the IRS on their Form 1099-B. And you have to deduct the effects of all these taxes to arrive at a true, after-all-tax yield.

Estate and Social Security Taxes

Municipals are included in estate calculations, and a tax may be due on their market value. Presently the estate tax threshold is rising from $600,000 to $1 million. After reaching that minimum, the rates are high. Estate planning is for experts.

Social Security beneficiaries have to include municipal bond interest in most income tax calculations, in effect paying some tax on state and local bonds. So some close figuring may be necessary to determine if naturally lower yielding municipals are right for such investors.

State Income Taxes

That's the good news—no federal tax on most state and local bond interest. But the bad news is that states are free to tax each other, and their levies often markedly reduce holders' out-of-state bond yields. As of 1999, forty-two states (all except Alaska, Indiana, Nevada, South Dakota, Texas, Utah, Washington, and Wyoming) levy some form of tax on out-of-state municipal bond interest. In addition, a few states tax their residents on the income from bonds issued by some of their own communities. By how much does state taxation reduce tax-exempt yields? For a rough rule of a thumb, multiply the applicable state tax bracket by an .05. So on an out-of-state municipal, a Maryland taxpayer now loses about 25 basis points (5% Maryland tax x .05 = .25%).

There is one set of bonds immune to any income taxes at all—federal, state, or local. The interest on bonds of U.S. affiliated issuers, primarily Puerto Rico but also including the Virgin Islands and some Pacific territories, is exempt by an Act of Congress dating back to 1917. So in Oregon, New Jersey, and all the other states, an apparent 5% on a Puerto Rico bond is a real 5%, 100% tax-free. Some managers have taken advantage of this provision. For example, 7.4% of Merrill Lynch's giant New York Municipal Bond Fund was originally placed in Puerto Rico electric, highway, and other of that island commonwealth's bonds.

Part Two

The Bonds

6

Bond Features

Bonds are the main form of a somewhat broader category, *fixed income investments,* other forms of which include bank certificates of deposit, preferred stock, and commercial paper. Fixed income investments are like IOUs, with rates of return and principal repayment dates agreed to in advance. This differentiates them from stocks and other *equity investments,* whose returns may vary and have no set date of redemption or fixed principal amount.

Principal Denominations

What is principal? Whether it's called face, par, or principal amount, it's how much an issuer promises to pay the investor at maturity. Most tax-exempts are originally priced somewhere near par (100% of principal). However, some come out at a discount (below par) and some at a premium (above par). Anyway, the principal amount is what will eventually be paid, 100 cents on the dollar.

Municipals used to sell in $1,000 denominations (units) of their principal, but the standard tax-exempt piece is now $5,000, and they trade in multiples of that amount. In practice, what difference does it make what denomination a bond comes in? Very little. It's like eggs, where two half-cartons and one whole carton both contain a dozen. One hundred bonds means $100,000, whether or not evidenced by twenty pieces of paper. However, bond jargon dies hard, and when we say "a bond," we mean $1,000. "Ten bonds" is $10,000 principal amount, "fifty bonds" means $50,000, "a hundred" is $100,000 worth, and "nine hundred ninety-five" is $995,000. After that it jumps. We say "a million" for $1 million worth and "5 million" when we're lucky enough to trade $5 million, and so forth.

Interest

Bond issues are sometimes referred to by their official birthday, their *dated date*, usually one close to when they were originally offered. Their first interest period often begins at the dated date, but not always.

Most municipal bonds pay interest twice a year, usually once on the same month and day the bonds are due and once six months later. So if a bond's maturity date is 7/1/17 you can expect it to pay interest every July 1 and on its twin, January 1, through 2017. How do you figure the exact amount of interest a bond will pay each six months? Logically, by multiplying the principal amount by the interest rate and dividing by two. So if we're looking at 100 Oregon 5% bonds, you don't have to be a math wizard to multiply $100,000 principal times the 5% rate (.05) to get to $5,000. Taking half of that (for the semiannual interest) brings you the answer: $2,500.

Suppose the Oregons were 7 1/2s. What would they pay every six months? $7,500? No. Half of that, $3,750. And on what days of the year? Hint: we call this particular pair of dates M and N1. And to figure the exact amount of accrued interest on any trade, just push the right buttons on your handy bond calculator, as we'll get to in the next chapter.

Bond Forms

Before 1980, most new bond issues were printed up and delivered physically, resulting in an enormous volume of (literally) paperwork. Now this has been largely replaced by the *book entry* system, whereby securities exist only as records of the issuer or its agents. Nothing physical at all, no thousands of pieces of paper shuffling around the country. What happens when a book entry bond is sold? Individual parts of each issue are transferred between owners by a system of electronic debits and credits. One nice feature of book entry is its ability to carve bond lots into any available multiple of $5,000. So if someone buys 75 bonds from a dealer, the registrar simply subtracts that amount from the dealer's holding and adds it to the investor's. Despite all the conveniences, some issues, particularly smaller, local ones, are still delivered in the old-fashioned, physical form, accommodating investors who prefer to see what they get.

Bearer Form

Formerly, principal ownership was usually evidenced by anonymous *bearer* bonds. Bearer, or coupon, bonds are physical pieces of paper stating that whoever presents them to the obligor at maturity gets paid the principal amount. Attached to bearer bonds are small coupons—one for each of the interest dates. A holder can cut off (clip) and deposit them into a checking account, and the bank sends them to the issuer's paying agent for credit. All in all, a cumbersome and expensive process, now largely supplanted by the book entry and registered mechanism.

Registered

In their *South Carolina* 1988 ruling the Supreme Court upheld Congress's decree prohibiting the issuance of tax-exempt bearer bonds. Thereafter, all municipals had to be registered. What is a registered bond? One, whether physical or book entry, where the name of the holder is recorded on the books of the *registrar,* who, upon proper documentation, will transfer that ownership to a new owner, again registered. Interest is also recorded and automatically sent out to holders. Book entry and registration are logical developments in our market, making it easier for principal and interest to flow between issuer and owner—also for the IRS to see who's doing what.

Bond Description

How do dealers keep track of all of the thousands of different bond descriptions? Chiefly by the CUSIP (Committee for Uniform Security Identification Procedure) number, provided by Standard & Poor's. S&P assigns an alpha number to all new emissions, overwhelmingly for municipals. So the first six digits of the CUSIP number for all Massachusetts Water Resource Authority bonds are 576049, and their particular 7% bonds due 4/1/98 were tagged 576049AR1.

How do you properly identify and describe a bond offering? By stating its principal amount, the exact security, coupon rate, maturity and call, and price and/or yield. In addition, written confirmations must include the CUSIP. Such as:

CUSIP	Amount	Bond	Coupon	Maturity	Yield	Price
686071AA3	100M	Oregon	4%	11/1/17ca	5.25%	84 3/4

What does that "M" after 100 mean? One thousand, from the Roman numeral. As we said, the old $1,000 denomination still prevails. What is the security behind these bonds? Oregon's full faith and credit. Revenue bonds must be so described. So, unless otherwise stated, a buyer can assume a bond is a G.O.

Call Features

What does that "ca" after 11/1/17 mean? Callable. Although the Oregon bonds may stay outstanding until 2017, the state reserves the right to prepay them before then. So you can't be sure exactly when you'll get repaid on a callable bond. When and at what price they may be earlier redeemed is part of the original bond issuing contract. Such as "on or after November 1, 2007 at a premium of 3%." Note that Oregon *may* call them but is definitely *not* obligated to; it's up to them.

Holders of these 4% Oregons can expect them to run to maturity. Bought at 84 3/4 ($84,750 principal), they will return a yield to maturity of 5.25%. What if the coupon were 5 1/2%—would they be worth more or less than 88 3/4? Obviously more. We return to pricing in the next chapters.

7

Dollar Pricing

So bonds sell in $5,000 units but are treated as $1,000s. Do we use these awkwardly big numbers? No. We price bonds using two abbreviated systems, one quantifying their principal and one their total return. The first is called *dollar pricing.* We will get to *yield pricing* in the next chapter.

In dollar pricing "100" stands for a bond's full principal amount. Ten bonds at 100 cost $10,000, a hundred bonds $100,000, and so on. Bonds priced in dollars are easy to understand and sell, and we offer them at the simplest price of all, 100 (par), as often as possible. (It's written "100" or "100 1/2" but spoken "par." Anyone who says "one hundred," or "one hundred and a half" is totally out of it.)

As the market goes up and down, so do bond prices. We measure their market value by applying straightforward percentages to their face amount, like 100, 99, 97, 94%, etc. Up 1% from par is 101, and down 1% is 99, or $990 per $1,000 principal amount. So ten bonds at 99 cost $9,900, a hundred cost $99,000, a million $990,000, and so on, always as percentages of $1,000.

Pop quiz: What does a dollar price of 85 stand for?
  Answer: $850.
Q: What do ten bonds at 85 cost?
  A: $8,500.

Points and Fractions

One percent of a bond's principal we call one *point.* How much is a point worth? Ten dollars ($1,000 x .01 = $10). So if you make a point on 25 bonds you have a $250 profit. And if you lose half a point on 100 bonds you have a $500 loss. As the market changes, bonds continue to be valued in dollar prices, up or down. Suppose a bond that was priced at 77 is later marked up to 78. We say it's up a point though that particular $10 is more than 1% of market value (1/77 = 1.3%).

Although points are precise enough for many purposes, competitive pressures compel us to divide them into fractions, usually in eighths (one-eighth of 1%, or $1.25 per bond). So get secure on your decimal equivalents, because bond calculators don't take them. Some competitors go beyond eighths, where we have to work even more finely, in dimes and even cents per bond.

Comparing Values

If you can buy the same cheese at two equally convenient stores, it's price that counts. Similarly, you can use dollar prices to evaluate different bond offerings. If two identical bonds are offered at differing prices the lower one obviously provides the better value. So if you saw two bond offerings like this:

CUSIP	Amount	Bond	Coupon	Maturity	Price
686000AA3	100 M	Oregon	5%	11/1/17ca	88 1/4
666000AA3	100 M	Oregon	5%	11/1/17ca	88.72

picking the better value is simple.

Dollar Bonds

Tax-exempt issues, particularly revenue bonds, are often designed so that many of their bonds bear the same coupon and same maturity date. When they reach the secondary market they used to be called *dollar bonds* because using percentages greatly simplified trading in them. At present they are usually called *actives,* because so many trade in yield.

Dollar prices also come in handy as a constant between bonds carrying different interest rates. When two similar bonds are offered at the same price, it's easy to see that the one with the higher coupon is the better investment:

Amount	Bond	Coupon	Maturity	Price
100 M	Hawaii	5%	11/1/17ca	98 1/4
100 M	Hawaii	5.1%	11/1/17ca	98 1/4

Here we have two bonds, identical except for coupon, at the same price. The one carrying the higher coupon is definitely the better buy.

Accrued Interest

As mentioned, when you buy a fixed income security, in addition to the dollar price, another amount, the *accrued interest* is ordinarily added on. On both its interest payment dates (such as May and November 1 in the Hawaii example) you start fresh and pay zero accrued interest. However, on any other date, a seller who has held it x number of days since the last paying date deserves the interest that has accrued (accumulated) in that period. Here time is literally money. Interest accrues daily, and when a sale is made between interest dates it is divided between the buyer and the seller, splitting it fairly. So a confirmation on 25 bonds sold at 102 might read $25,500 principal plus $333.33 accrued interest, for a total of $25,833.33.

Our bond interest year has the usual twelve months, but with one neat twist. Every municipal month, even February, is assigned exactly thirty days, and interest accrues on a uniform 360 day calendar, leap years and common years alike. A 7.20% bond pays $72 per $1,000 per year, which is $6 every month. Six dollars a month divided by 30 days is twenty cents a day. So if you have been holding $50,000 worth of 7.20% bonds and sell them 10 days after you were paid a coupon, you get ten days times twenty cents a day, or $2 per bond interest. And if a new investor buys them on the same day, she pays the same $2, dividing the interest between seller and buyer. Fifty bonds at 98 comes to $49,000 principal, plus $100 accrued interest, for a total of $49,100.

Current Yield

Amount	Bond	Coupon	Maturity	Price	Current Yield
25M	Georgia	5	5/1/18	100	5.00%
500M	Georgia	5	5/1/18	101	4.95
1,000M	Georgia	5	5/1/18	101.50	4.93
475M	Louisiana	5	4/1/19	96	5.21
50M	Louisiana	5	4/1/19	95.50	5.24

Figure 2

Let's look at the above table. You see it has a column for *current yields.* If someone buys the twenty-five Georgia 5% bonds at 100 and holds them to maturity they will receive 5.00% a year, or $5 for every $100 invested. This return rate is its current yield, 5.00% the first year, 5.00% the next, right up to 2018. It's the *now* yield, every single year. Current yield is sometimes used to calculate the return on municipals, but more often on common stocks and other investments that, unlike bonds, have no maturity. In fact, its other name is *stock yield,* which you can see every day in the newspaper stock tables.

How is current yield figured? Divide coupon by dollar price. At 100 (the whole thing, or 1.00) it's easy—anything divided by 1 is itself. So the current on a 4.00% bond is 4.00%, on a 4 1/2% bond 4.50%, etc.

What happens at prices over 100, on *premium bonds*? For example take the 500 Georgias at a higher price—101. Divide 5% by 1.01 and you get 4.95%, the current yield. The buyer still gets $5 per year per $100 invested, but since the amount of money invested is higher, the return on it is lower. Only common sense—if a bond at 100 returns 5.00%, it will return less at 101. And at 101 1/2 the return is lower still, a 4.93% current. So, *the current yield of a premium bond is always lower than its coupon.* And as the dollar price goes up, the current yield goes down.

To finish the picture, bonds selling under 100 are called *discount* bonds and the *current on a discount bond is always higher than its coupon.* To find out how much higher, again divide the coupon by the dollar price. As the price goes down, the yield goes up—here to a 5.21% and a 5.24%.

A fundamental of investing has surfaced right here—*prices*

and yields move inversely, that is, in opposite directions. This applies to all securities—bonds, stocks, trusts, funds, etc. So *when prices go up, yields go down.* And *when prices go down, yields go up,* automatically. Price up? Yield down. You can't get away from it.

So that's current yield. But if an investor holds a premium bond to its maturity at 100, he will have a paper loss. How do losses on premium bonds (and gains on discount bonds) enter the current yield equation? They don't. Current is just the now yield, telling the whole story only at 100. For a more complete gauge of income we must march on to yield to maturity.

8

Yield Pricing

Yield to Maturity

Our second pricing system, *yield to maturity,* provides a more complete picture of bond return. A complex equation factors in coupon, dollar price, time to maturity, and also gains or losses, solving for *yield to maturity.* We shorten it to *yield,* expressed in one annual percentage rate (APR), 5.00%, 4.25%, 5.55%, and so on. So a bond *priced to yield* a 5.50% will return a five and a half percent average annual return over the life of the investment.

And that's just the way we say it—*priced to yield.* Why? Because every bond offered at a certain yield has its own dollar price equivalent, as we shall be exploring shortly. Just to make sure—when we say *yield,* we mean yield to maturity. When, occasionally, current yield does come up, specify it. For instance, you might say correctly, "At a five forty-five, those Washingtons' current yield is only a four."

Lots of people buy bank certificates of deposit, but don't ask me why. They're illiquid and fully taxable and usually return less than Treasuries. However, imagine a customer has bought a $10,000 5% twelve month C.D. After a year you'd expect him to get his $10,000 back along with $500 interest. However, if somehow he had bought the same $10,000 C.D. at a $100 discount, at $9,900, naturally his total return ($500 interest + $100 gain) would be higher than 5%. And if he had paid more than $10,000, its return would be lower, for the same reasons, in reverse. Figuring the yield on discount (below 100) or premium (priced above 100) bonds works similarly. So a 5% bond bought at 99 has to yield more than 5.00%, and bought at a premium less than

5.00%. You could calculate it yourself via the yield equation, but I wouldn't recommend it. Fortunately, our bond calculators easily figure any given yield to maturity.

We saw in the last chapter how dollar prices cut principal into large ten-dollar points and then into dollars, dimes, and cents. How do we denominate yield? First in percents, each expressing 1% of annual *income*. The difference between a bond at a 6.00% yield and one at a 5.00% is 1 percent of annualized return. And moving from a 5.00% down to a 4.00% also reduces yield by 1 percent.

However, in municipals you seldom see interest rates swing that much. For convenience we divide each percentage into 100 parts—.01s, spoken "oh-ones." Each of these hundredths we call one *basis point*. Why? I don't know. But that's what everybody calls them—basis points. So from a 5.00% to a 4.99% is a move of one basis point, and so is the change from a 3.75% to a 3.76%. *Basis points* and most particularly their multiples of five (*oh-fives*) are among the most frequently used terms in the municipal business. Why? Like the five-minute marks on a clock face, the .05 has usually proven our handiest yield increment.

Before we go on, let's recognize the confusion that may arise between two of our key terms—*points* and *basis points*. One point is 1 percent of principal, or $10 per $1,000 bond. Now *basis* points? One-hundredth percent of yield? To keep them straight, remember that points are big—$10 per bond. But basis points are measly little hundredths of a percentage of yield. When we hear: "Bonds are up a point!" we know their dollar price is up $10 per bond, a hefty amount. But when we mean basis points, we say, "The second bid was just one basis point away, a 5.45 and a 5.46%," maybe only about 75 cents a bond. Now, let's see exactly how changing a bond's price changes its yield.

Current Yield and Yield to Maturity

S.D.4/1/1999

	Amount	Bond	Coupon	Maturity	Price	Current Yield	Yield to Maturity
#1	200M	Summit, NJ	5%	4/1/2000	100	5.00%	5.00%
#2	200M	Summit, NJ	5	4/1/2000	99	5.05	6.05
#3	200M	Summit, NJ	5	4/1/2000	101	4.95	3.97
#4	100M	St. Louis, MO	4	4/1/00	98	4.08	6.09
#5	100M	St. Louis, MO	4	4/1/07	98	4.08	4.30

Figure 3

Discount Bond Yield

Figure 3 begins with three lines, but just one bond description: \$200,000 principal amount of Summit, New Jersey, 5% bonds due April 1, 2000, just one year after the settlement date of April 1, 1999. In line #1, the Summits are priced at 100, where, because there will be neither gain nor loss, they yield their coupon, 5.00% to maturity. As we said earlier, a bond priced at 100 always yields its coupon. Lower the price to 99, and the yield rises to 6.05%. Why? For two reasons: (1.) The discount holder gets the same 5.00% coupon as the 100 owner but has less money invested, as shown by the slightly higher current yield. (2.) More important, the discount buyer will receive a \$2,000 gain in just one year (200 bonds x \$10 = \$2,000). As the price goes down, the yield goes up, or as the professors say, price and yield move inversely. Note that this also applies to current yield. However, while the current barely budges, YTM jumps 1.05%.

Why do some bonds sell at discounts? Supply and demand. Suppose comparable 6% bonds suddenly became available at 100. Who would buy old Summit 5s bonds at the same price? No one. The market soon lowers their price until they provide a yield competitive to the new, higher rates.

Premium Bond Yield

Premium bond yields move very much like discounts, only in the opposite direction. Priced above 100, their yield is always lower than their coupon. (1.) Because their current yield is lower. (2.) Because their holder will lose the premium paid when the bonds mature down at 100. From the point of view of a buyer, when Summit 5s were trading near 100 a block of comparable 6% bonds would certainly be worth more. Naturally it's better to get sixty dollars per year rather than fifty dollars. So the 6s would sell higher than 100, perhaps at 101, where they would also yield about a 5.00% to maturity, equaling things up. From a holder's side, the same logic applies—an investor owning 6s wouldn't sell them at the same price 5s were selling at. He would want, and deserve, more. Now let's see how yield figures in time.

Time Effect

Figure 3, lines 4 and 5 show two bonds with the same coupon and dollar price, but two vastly different yields to maturity. Why? The time differential. Number 4 is due in one year, and number 5 is due in eight years. The one-year buyer gets a 6.09% yield, while the eight-year buyer only gets a 4.29%. Although the coupon and the price are the same, one holder receives his $2,000 profit (100 x $20) much sooner, and yield to maturity shows the result of this advantage clearly. In mathematical terms, yield to maturity is a function of coupon, price, and also time.

One fine point before we move on: When we say "*a* five," we mean a yield of 5.00%. *Yield to maturity is understood, but not stated.* So to say it right, it's *a* "five" or *a* "five oh-five," with the "a" standing for "a yield of." If you said, "the Cals are at five," you would sound very unprofessional, because "five" without the "a" in front of it means a dollar price of 5. When we mean at a dollar price of 5, or 55, we say just "at five" or "at fifty-five," with no "a." *A* fifty-five would mean a yield of 55.00%, quite a different proposition. If there's a chance of misunderstanding, say "a five basis," to emphasize that you mean a yield, not a dollar price.

Price Shopping

Since yield to maturity describes a bond's return accurately, it can serve as an excellent gauge for comparing the value of bonds with different coupon rates and prices. It's obviously better to pay 100 for a bond than 101 and better to buy 5s rather than comparable 4 1/2s at the same price. But choosing between two offerings, one of which carries both a lower coupon and also a lower dollar price, may not be easy, even for pros.

Suppose you saw two offerings of the same bond, say Seattles due out fourteen years. One is a 5 1/2 priced at 100, while the other is 4% priced at 83.58. Comparing them by yield is the sort of job traders do every bond market hour, if not more often. Other things equal, which is the better buy, the 5 1/2s at 100 or the 4s at a big discount? You might answer, "The one with the higher yield to maturity," and that's right. But which one is it? It's like shopping at the supermarket, where you have to choose a dozen and a half oranges at $3.98 or three pounds for $1.59. The 5 1/2s have the higher coupon, but what about the 4s' lower price? To decide, we figure the yield on the 4s and see if it's higher than the 5.50% yield we know 5 1/2s provide at 100.

From Dollars to Yield

To find the yield equivalent of a known dollar price, first enter into whatever computer system you have the correct *settlement date* (S.D.). What is an S.D.? The day bonds and money will change hands, on, as a rule, T+3, or three business days after the trade date (the day the trade was done). Then you enter the bond's coupon, maturity, and price and push the right button, and out comes the answer in a flash. In this case, first enter 4/1/99 and push S.D. Then 4, and push COUPON. 4/1/13 and MAT. 83.58 and TO YIELD, and out it comes. Answer? A 5.72% yield. A 4% bond due in fourteen years at a price of 83.58 yields 5.72% to maturity. In goes coupon, time, and price; out comes yield. The 4s yield twenty-two basis points more than the 5 1/2s.

Value of the .05

Coupon	Maturity	Yield	$ Price	Value of .05
5	1 year	@4.95%	100.047	
		@5.00	100.000	
			.048	48 cents/$1,000
5	2 years	@4.95	100.094	
		@5.00	100.000	
			.094	94 cents
5	3 years	@4.95	100.137	
		@5.00	100.000	
			.137	$1.13
5	5 years	@4.95	100.219	
		@5.00	100.000	
			.219	$2.19
5	10 years	@4.95	100.390	
		@5.00	100.000	
			.390	$3.90
5	20 years	@4.95	100.630	
		@5.00	100.000	
			.630	$6.30
5	20 years	@6.40	84.330	
		@6.45	83.834	
			.494	$4.94
6	30 years	@5.95	100.695	
		@6.00	100.000	
			.695	$6.95
7	30 years	@6.95	100.626	
		@7.00	100.000	
			.626	$6.26

Figure 4

From Yield to Dollars

Suppose you start with a yield. How do you find the dollar price? Enter settlement, coupon, and maturity. Then enter the yield and push TO PRICE. In the same example, 4/1/99, 4, 4/1/13, 5.72, TO PRICE, and out comes 83.58. Nothing to it.

Value of the .05

We can also convert yield *changes,* such as by one .05, into dollars. After all, you can't spend an .05, but dollars always come in handy. Figure 4 shows 6s priced at a 6.00%. What happens in dollars if the trader who owns them marks them up an .05, so that they now yield a 5.95? They go up about $7 a bond, moving from 100 up to 100.696. Traders would say that this .05 is worth seven dollars.

We saw that the value of a point is always $10, half of that, $5, and so on. Is the value of the .05 always the same—$5, for instance?

No. A rough rule of thumb is that the .05 is 50 cents in one year, $1 in two, 1/4 point in 5, 3/8 in ten, and out to $7 a bond on the long end. The more curious of you readers may see that the value of the .05 goes up with maturity, and up with dollar price, but *down* with coupon. The longer the maturity, the higher the dollar price, and the lower the coupon, the higher the .05. Formally, yield changes vary with maturity and dollar price, and inversely to coupon. For another thumb rule, think 16 to 4 to 1. When one .05 may change sixteen times more than another according to a bond's maturity, dollar price will change it four times more and coupon only one. As you see, learning about municipals is something like learning English—its oddities make it tough to get to know, but once you have it, it's special. And by the way, when you get proficient in municipals, you can usually find a job almost anywhere in the United States—it's a readily portable skill.

Premium Bonds and Yield to Call

On most days we see bonds offered with coupons higher than those currently available. These will naturally cost more than comparable bonds at today's rates. However, most of these can be called in, that is, redeemed by their issuers before final maturity. Sometimes these call provisions will be at premium prices, 103, for instance, but often the issuer may redeem them at 100. (Technically speaking, if a bond is redeemable at a premium over principal we say it's "callable," while if redeemable at 100, it's "optional.") In addition, most call provisions extend over many years, with changing features. A common form makes bonds callable in ten years at 103, with premiums declining by 1/4 point every six months, finally reaching and remaining at 100 for the ten years remaining until maturity.

The true yield of such redeemable bonds can be accurately figured using a variant of YTM, *yield to call.* At a time when municipals are selling readily at 5.00%, you may see a 7% bond issued in palmier days offered at 110. If this gives a yield to maturity of 6.00%, it apparently offers an investor a good deal. However, looking more closely, if, in fact, the issuer calls the bonds in at its first opportunity, say in two years at a price of 103, then her yield might only be a 4.18%. The YTC formula figures in the effects of coupon income, current yield, loss of 7 points (from 110 down to 103), and the time factor, producing the 4.18%.

How are we required to offer any bond? At the *lowest yield* that an investor could possibly get, whether the issuer redeems the bonds on any of their call dates or lets them run to maturity. In this case? At a 4.18%, figured to the two-year call at 103. If the bonds don't get called, the buyer will get more than a 4.18%, but in no case less, and you have both correctly described them and protected yourself.

So that's that for pricing bonds. But what about the bonds themselves? Aren't some stronger than others, and some weaker? Yes, of course. Let's go on to see how to determine a bond's strength, to credit analysis.

9

Tax-Backed Bond Credit Analysis

Ability and Willingness to Pay

Boiled down to essentials, municipal bond credit analysis is an investigation of an issuer's *ability and willingness to pay. Ability* is measured chiefly by economics, *willingness* by social and political factors.

The Credit Analyzers

Who actually does this credit detective work? Chiefly municipal bond analysts employed by investors, dealers, and financial service companies. Large investors such as the Vanguard funds, Allstate Insurance Company, and Chase Bank maintain their own municipal research departments to approve or disapprove bonds their investment people may buy. Also to monitor bonds in existing portfolios for signs of credit change. Many larger dealers also employ research staffs to analyze individual bonds and to appraise whole classes of issues (like public power or housing bonds). Finally, three proprietary service organizations, Moody's, Standard & Poor's, and Fitch, collect fees for grading tens of thousands of municipal and other securities. They also publish and sell opinions on a wide range of credit topics. See Chapter 19 where we cover raters in more detail.

Prices and Quality

But don't jump to the conclusion that credit analysis alone sets bond prices. Prices and interest rates are determined by investor demand interacting with current issuer and dealer supply. And these levels are determined by the current general interest rate structure. So when U.S. Treasuries in a certain year yield 7.00%, most tax-exempts will be priced somewhere between 6.00% and 6.50%, depending on their quality.

G.O.s and Revs

General obligation bonds are backed by an issuer's full faith and credit, payable from all sources, usually including real estate taxes. And revenue bonds are backed solely from specific streams of municipal enterprise income. Formerly this produced a clear and simple two-layer cake. However, the increasing interdependence of federal, state, and local governments and the mandates for social change have created a much more complex system. In response, the market has developed new types of bonds—many also tax-backed, but not pure G.O.s. So today it's more like a marble cake.[1] However, let's begin with straight general obligations. After all, every year municipalities issue well over $50 billion worth of these plain vanilla bonds.

Binding Obligations

Before looking at credit numbers, it's essential to make sure that any bond represents a legal, enforceable debt. And as I write, the marketplace is discovering three whole series of questionably issued, non-rated, but supposedly tax-exempt obligations that municipal bond dealers sold to the public. Especially when a bond is nonrated it's vital to check it out. Where can you find proof of a bond's validity and its tax status? If you're a professional analyst, you scrutinize the original issuing documents.

But for most of us, a recognized bond attorney's *legal opinion* is sufficient. See Chapter 18 for more on this crucial document.

Real Estate Values

How do cities raise the money to cover the cost of their operations? First and foremost, by levying (charging) taxes on the real estate within their boundaries. In fact, property taxes provide about half a typical pure G.O. issuer's income. Municipalities periodically assess (estimate) the dollar value of each parcel of land and its improvements. Then the governing body votes one or more *ad valorem* (according to the value) tax rates against these assessments. So if in one block there are four houses assessed at \$100,00, \$125,000, \$150,000 and \$170,000 and one store on the corner at \$250,000, and the *ad valorem* rate is 2.152%, they would each owe that percentage of their assessments. This would come to yearly totals of \$2,152, \$2,690, \$3,228, and \$5,380, respectively.

These tax bills are sent out to property owners, who give them a high payment priority. Why? Because municipalities automatically acquire a lien on property against unpaid taxes, and they can and do seize the real estate and sell it. So bonds backed this way are well secured indeed.

Municipalities use assessed valuation to figure tax bills. However, A.V. is often lower than market value, by unequal margins in various states. Therefore, we often substitute *true value,* T.V., giving bond buyers a more accurate and uniform picture.

Overall Debt and True Value

Analysts heavily emphasize one pure G.O figure—it's O.D./T.V., or the ratio of its overall debt to the real estate's true value. *Overall debt* is the total amount of debt an issuing community has promised to service. How do you calculate this? First, take its *gross debt* (all its outstanding bonds and notes) and subtract any offsetting items such as reserves and surpluses, to arrive at its *net debt.* Next, add the share the issuer bears of other government obligations—its *overlapping debt.* This may be its proportionate slice of county bonded debt or of other obligors, such as a consolidated school district.

O.D./T.V. produces the simplest ratio of G.O. bond's credit strength. All other factors being equal, the lower this percentage, the stronger the bond. For example, in 1997 AAA issuer Dallas, Texas showed a low O.D./T.V. ratio of 2.9%. And Ft. Worth and Houston, both AA, figured to 4.4% and 5.1%, while Round Rock and Grapevine, A rated, came in at 6.0% and 6.5%. Then, Lockhart and Allen ISD, BBB Texas names, had higher percentages, 10.4%, and 15.3%, respectively. These figures tie into national averages, where an O.D./T.V. ratio of less than 5% usually indicates a higher quality bond and where over 10% raises a warning signal.

Per Capita Debt

A second calculation fleshes out G.O. debt figures. Again take the overall bond amount, and divide by the population count, to produce a *per capita* (by the head) figure. In general, the lower the number, the higher the quality of the issuer. In 1997 the per capita debt of the same seven Texas issuers figured at $1,274; $1,254; $2,001; $2,555; $5,835; $1,709; and $5,114, respectively.

However, tax-exempt bond analysis isn't accomplished strictly by formula. Suppose a city had almost no debt and a healthy property value? If this means that it has skimped on public facilities, the community may deteriorate and property values decline. Or, if instead it decides to restore its infrastructure, it may have to borrow heavily, keeping residents happy, and also attracting new ones. So a balanced position, where a municipality maintains public facilities properly, while avoiding overbuilding, is highly desirable. One benchmark of this balance is the percentage of municipal income spent on debt service. Something like 10% is ideal in many circumstances.

State G.O.s

The U.S. Constitution gives states *sovereign powers,* which complicate analyzing their bonds' credit. On the one hand, state legislatures can act in ways local governments can't. On the other, voters often tie states' hands with initiatives and referenda, sharply limiting their powers. We see this in the many well-known state propositions. And it's hard to predict what restrictions will come next. In addition, few states levy property taxes, instead securing their bonds by pledging receipts from their other sources, including income, sales, and other taxes. So state G.O.s have to be carefully and individually examined, especially stressing the political and social elements.

Other Tax-Backed Bonds

O.D./T.V. and per capita debt provide a handy thumbnail picture of the creditworthiness of a pure G.O. Then, going deeper, especially for non-pure G.O.s, we add in the other factors—economic, financial, and management—to arrive at an overall credit judgment. The further removed a G.O. bond is from plain vanilla, for instance in one that will be paid only from future appropriations, the more we have to examine the background components.

In addition, many other governmental units have issued various types of contingently tax-backed securities. Prominent among them are *certificates of participation (COPS),* and local moral obligation bonds. Most of these have paid off as expected. However, as S & P's Criteria points out, it is particularly necessary to determine the underlying viability of projects financed this way.

Double-Barreled

Over the years thousands of towns and cities have constructed and continue to operate water, sewer, electric, and other enterprises. Often they finance these utilities with *double-barreled* bonds. Serviced by the project net income, they are also backed by the community's general obligation pledge. And Double Barrel Avenue is a busy two-way street. When the enterprise generates more net income than required to service the bonds, the excess typically goes back to the city. So, general obligation, double-barreled, and moral obligation bonds are involved, in different ways, with an issuer's main checkbook—its *general fund.* Property taxes and other income flow into a general fund, which is used to pay pure G.O. debt service. Moral obligations may also be paid out of this fund, if appropriated. And double-barreled bonds may either draw on it or contribute to it, a two-way street.

U.T.s and L.T.s

Most issuers sell G.O.s payable from property taxes, which are unlimited as to rate or amount. These we call *unlimited tax* or U.T.s. However, some municipalities are bound by laws that limit, or cap, their property tax levies. These we call *limited tax,* or L.T.s. In practice, I've never seen a G.O. default because of a tax limitation, and U.T.s and L.T.s now trade practically identically.

Tax-Increment and Special District Bonds

Continuing to adapt to the marble caking of America, many states have authorized cities to create special districts within their own bounds and to sell tax-backed bonds to finance improvements in these areas. Some are organized as *tax-increment districts,* which sell bonds to improve water and sewer, road, and other systems. This separately identified real estate is then assessed periodically, and the district levies a tax only on any growth above a designated base year. Other units are organized as *special districts,* where a variety of property taxes support bonds sold to develop an emerging district's facilities—for instance, the many California Mello-Roos special district bonds.

Leases

Many states have enacted bond enabling legislation so restrictive that their localities can't issue enough G.O.s to meet basic needs. So, for instance, hundreds of Pennsylvania and Indiana communities have resorted to selling bonds, even for schools, that are technically *lease revenues* but in practice are treated as if they were G.O.s.

Bonds backed by leases on less essential facilities such as those to construct stadiums, convention, or health care centers are quite different. Investors know that leases can be broken and should a nonvital or obsolete project fall out of community favor it might try to forfeit its obligation. (In fact, two municipalities have recently balked at paying—in both cases for unpopular facilities—and more may come along.) Therefore, analysts first look closely at how necessary a project is and whether or not the community is solidly behind it. Then they examine the terms of the lease itself, to see what legal recourse bondholders would have if the money were not appropriated or delayed.

Often these projects are so essential and so noncontroversial that the raters will rank them on a par with the issuer's G.O. debt. In other cases, the lease rating will fall one slot below. But so far, so good, with lease revenue bonds—nearly all have repaid their trusting investors as promised.

Moral Obligation

When voters object to financing a highly specialized facility through a G.O. bond issue, politicians may resort to floating *moral obligation bonds*. Moral obs usually fund a project meant to be self-supporting but as yet untested. For example, the first such issuer, New York State, sold several series of housing and health care bonds, each designed to pay its own way. However, they were sold with the specification that should the project fail to generate enough income, timely application would be made to the New York legislature to replenish the bonds' reserve fund in amounts sufficient to repay bondholders. And in fact this drawdown has occurred for at least three moral obligation issues.

Many states have established other kinds of obligations, such as bond banks, which are backed by similar future contingency appropriation pledges. There are now about $8 billion outstanding, the vast majority covered by their own revenues. The rating services usually assign state moral obs one rank below an issuer's straight G.O.s.

Economic Factors

Although debt ratios provide a good barometer of the current strength of a bond, the community economic base will likely determine its future creditworthiness. In addition, the state and regional situation affects the local picture. A strong overall base often allows a city to provide sufficient services and for their continued maintenance. A weak base may mean area deterioration, loss of appearance and property value, and a decline in population. What are some factors studied? The citizen age, education levels, their employment skills, and particularly their income and wealth figures.

Then, returning to property values, we examine the quality of the tax base, to see what proportion is from the residential, commercial, and industrial components. If a few leading taxpayers provide a particularly large part of the property tax base, then we analyze their economic and financial strength and their commitment to the community. For instance, Kenosha, Wisconsin, is definitely a Daimler/Chrysler town, and despite its conservative financial practices, its lenders may well keep a wary eye on the auto industry.

Financial Factors

If a community manages its strengths well and provides for shortcomings, then it can probably withstand sudden changes or even meet emergencies. Key positive indicators of financial adeptness include: (1.) adherence to generally accepted accounting principles (GAAP); (2.) issuance of an audited Comprehensive Annual Financial Report (CAFR); and (3.) conformance to the Government Finance Officers Association (GFOA) standards. Also considered is the state of the balance sheet, especially the amount of available fund reserves should a rainy day suddenly hit. Also the patterns of short-term borrowing can reveal either prudence or stress.

Administrative Factors

Administrative factors add considerably to the overall assessment. A professional staff knowledgeable in the community affairs and ready with answers for analysts gives a fine impression. Factors considered are: how budgets are drawn and met, how sound the capital needs forecasts are, what the labor and pension situation is, and how well the community sets and meets its fee and assessment levels. For example, if a city actually collects 95% or more of its tax assessments and takes measures to attack delinquencies, then it looks as though the administrators are doing a good job.

Summary

As we mentioned, the principal job of G.O. analysis is to estimate a community's ability and willingness to pay. How do we figure the probability that the issuer will perform as promised? After all the facts and figures are in, we weigh the assets against the liabilities. Taking debt, economic, financial, and administrative elements into consideration, we balance the pluses against the minuses. Obviously this is part objective science and part subjective art.

In some cases, the community liabilities and other minuses are light and the assets relatively heavy. Their bonds get a high credit ranking, perhaps triple or double A by the raters. The highest rated bonds now comprise about 10% of all issues. (Not counting insured bonds, for which see Chapter 21.) If liabilities and assets seem to balance fairly evenly, we conclude that in all probability the bonds will pay off. These we give a medium-quality (A) credit ranking.

In cases where the liabilities seem to outweigh the assets, for example with an especially heavy debt load, or where income levels are low and declining, we conclude that in times of economic distress bond repayment would be threatened. The stronger ones of this category, something like 10% of all G.O.s, we might consider lower investment grade (BBB). Below this, maybe the weakest 2% of all G.O.s, would not qualify as standard investments.

Note

1. I am greatly indebted to Standard & Poor's *Public Finance Criteria,* New York, 1999, especially its tax-backed section. I highly recommend that any serious municipal bond participant study this practical and readable manual.

10

Revenue Bond Credit Analysis

As mentioned, most revenue bonds finance projects that benefit some, but not all, citizens in an issuing community. People use the facility in unequal measures and pay accordingly. So, if one family uses twice as much water, gas, or electricity as another, they will be billed about double. And if another family has its own well, it may pay nothing at all for city water.

Revenue Bond Purposes

Revenue bonds fall into five chief purpose categories: utility, transportation, housing, health and education, and corporation. *Utility* revs, backed by such traditional projects as water, sewer, and power facilities, were among the first to be issued. For example, San Antonio, Texas, has issued electric and gas revenue bonds since prewar days and enjoys both a good reputation and double-A ratings for them. In recent years newer forms of such municipal projects have been sold, including stadiums, telephone systems, nursing homes, and even racetracks. *Transportation* bonds, starting with one of the first, the Pennsylvania Turnpike, now include airport, bridge and tunnel, and port facility bonds. *Housing* bonds, for both single- and multifamily projects, though federally restricted in volume, still comprise a significant portion of revenue new issues. Genuine public-purpose *health and education bonds,* such as sold to finance Cleveland's famous Eye Clinic or the many facilities of the New York State Dormitory Authority, are among those most frequently issued. And *corporations* may back and sell tax-exempts, predominantly earmarked for environmental considerations. In addition, there are many miscellaneous revenue types such as those secured by excise taxes, governmental liquor sales, and even lottery profits.

The Analyzing Process

The first steps analysts take to determine a revenue bond's quality are very like those taken with a G.O. (1.) make sure the bond is a validly issued obligation; and (2.) ascertain that the source of payment is firmly dedicated to paying off this bond. Do property taxes enter here? No. Revenue bonds are payable only from defined and identified income streams, usually specifically *excluding* real estate taxes. That's their chief difference from G.O.s. Also, revs are *not* full faith and credit obligations, they are paid solely from designated and limited sources of income. In fact, revs are sometimes called *limited obligations.*

By the way, you may see a curve ball thrown at you here—sometimes revenue issuers say their bonds are general obligations, but only *of the authority,* going on to note that they have no taxing power. It would certainly make more sense if they phrased it differently, but here in the major leagues, curveballs are a fact of life.

The Credit Analysts

Investors, dealers, and the rating agencies are kept busy grading revenue issues of all types. They are often easier to assess than G.O.s, because with revs the economics of the situation dominate the analysis. You can measure a revenue bond's income stream, subtract expenses, and soon arrive at net income, giving you a good idea how well this stacks up against its debt service. As we saw with G.O.s, the imponderables of past and future political and social factors often enter the equation, making their analysis less scientific.

Revenue Bond Analysis

There are three stages in determining the strength of a validly issued revenue bond: (1.) examining the net income and the debt service of the enterprise in isolation from its setting; (2.) seeing how well the enterprise fits into its locale; and (3.) looking at the setting itself.

Income, Expense, and Debt Service

Revenue Bond Backing

Under corporation law, bondholders, due only a fixed return, take precedence over other classes of security owners if a company runs into financial difficulty. After them come preferred stockholders and, finally, common stock owners. So, when you are appraising the strength of the bonds of a publicly-owned utility such as Commonwealth Edison of Chicago, two factors leap out: (1.) how much money it makes; and (2.) how much it owes bondholders. Divide the first by the second to get the simplest test of how strong the bond is, its debt service *coverage.*

Let's take as an example a seasoned municipal issuer, Jacksonville, and one of its revenue bonds. For many years this northern Florida city has been issuing bonds to construct and expand its water and sewer facilities. What have the financial results looked like recently?

Income and Expense Jacksonville Water and Sewer System			
	Total Income	**Expense**	**Net Income**
1994	$ 95,660,000	$59,203,000	$36,457,000
1995	112,381,000	58,683,000	53,698,000
1996	124,279,000	60,671,000	63,608,000
1997	124,730,000	64,506,000	60,224,000
1998 (Est.)	132,000,000	67,000,000	65,000,000

Figure 5

Figure 5 shows that its income has grown steadily in the past few years. What does income include? All operating revenues, including interest earned. In the same years, expenses have stayed fairly steady. Expenses include all operating payments, amortization, and depreciation, *except debt service.* Why not debt service? Because that's the figure we use to calculate coverage. Total income minus expense gives net income.

Coverage			
Jacksonville Water and Sewer System			
	Net Income	**Debt Service**	**Coverage**
1994	$36,457,000	$14,458,000	2.52x
1995	53,698,000	15,000,000	3.58x
1996	63,608,000	15,541,000	4.09x
1997	60,224,000	20,257,000	2.97x
1998 (Est)	65,000,000	21,986,000	2.96x
Average			3.22x

Figure 6

In the above table we see this net income figure again, and some past and projected debt service requirements. Year by year we divide net income by D.S., producing the annual coverage figures shown in the last column. These range from 2.52 times up to 4.09 times, with an average of 3.22. This last number, average annual coverage, sums up in one number the ability to pay what is owed.

The Bond in Its Environment

Other factors mostly relate to the predictability of future coverage. Among these are how long the *record* of successful operation is, the *stability* of the enterprise type, *management* strength, how fully the system is *financed,* and the level of *user charges.*

As to the historical *record,* the longer the better, with five years providing an adequate time to assess a system's reliability. Newer or start-up projects are often less predictable and give analysts question marks instead of answers. *Stability* varies greatly from type to type: water and sewer at the top of the list, followed by most excise taxes, electric distribution systems, electric wholesale operations, port projects, health and education facilities, and airports. Bridge and tunnel projects often bring up the rear. Naturally these are generalities, but most revenue bonds conform to type.

Management strength, often apparent in talking to the municipal professionals themselves, may show in the quality and clarity of their periodic reports. Sometimes it's hard to estimate how fully a municipal enterprise is *financed.* However, interviews with the managers, plus a look at the frequency of past issues, especially short-term ones, may give a good idea. *User rate* levels can be compared to both national and state levels. Many states' utility commissions regulate municipal power and other charges, and their attitude toward rate increases should be considered, particularly in California. Also, these days the deregulation of private utilities may bring some surprises.

Summing up, negatives for revenue bonds are new or start-up systems, the more volatile kinds of service, weak management, frequent needs for additional financing, and high user fees. Also, analysts look at cash and reserve balances and the regularity of the flow of funds, as well as the additional bond clause, which states under what conditions more bonds backed by the same revenues may be issued.

The Setting

Is the strength of a community's G.O.s a factor to consider in ranking its revs? Yes, definitely. Why? Let's go back to the ability and willingness to pay. One prime element in assessing *ability* is the economic background, which affects both general obligations and revenues. And because the quality of full faith borrowing often indicates a community's *willingness* to pay. When does willingness come into play? Mostly in difficult times, the likes of which we haven't seen in many a moon.

So, the general economic background of the issuing community is the setting in which the revenue bond rests. Favorable factors include a steady or moderate population growth, a high level of personal income, and low and stable unemployment, also, such collateral items as the trend of bank deposits, construction permits, and utility usage.

Now that's the whole Jacksonville water and sewer picture: (1.) validly issued and tax-exempt; (2.) good coverage figures; and (3.) a record of successful operation. A traditional and stable purpose with experienced management. Now, suppose you decide, what would your rating be? I would say high, but not the highest. The strongest single factor is Jacksonville's continuing history of successful operation. But this utility is still in a growth phase, and this precludes it from the gilt-edge, highest possible rank, which is extremely rare on revenue bonds. Moody's, Standard & Poor's, and Fitch all agree, weighing in with Aa3, AA–, and AA—, respectively, or, as we write it, AA3/AA–/AA—.

Part Three

The Primary Market

11

Competitive Underwriting

So far we have covered how bonds originate and how to price and analyze them. Now it's time to see how these elements come together when dealers buy a new issue. First we'll talk about old-fashioned competitive underwriting, going on to negotiated deals in the next chapter.

In the 1990s U.S. municipalities have been selling some $200 billion worth of new issues a year. This total comprises more than 10,000 separate issues, or over 200 weekly. However, most attention is focused on the 20 or so issues a week of $10 million or more. They are listed in the *Bond Buyer*'s featured calendar and on many dealers' internal information sheets.

In recent years, only about one-quarter of the larger issues have been sold via public bidding, with the remainder selling by negotiation. What about the smaller issues, the ones less than $10 million? These range from smaller sales by larger municipalities down to tiny issues of local interest. If you take out your *Bond Buyer* and a magnifying glass, you'll see issues sold to finance a single school bus or a few fire hydrants. Naturally these draw more attention from locally minded dealers and investors.

The Dealer Middlemen

All of the larger and many smaller tax-exempt dealers regularly *underwrite* competitive new issues. The largest underwriters are organized as separate departments of publicly owned firms such as Morgan Stanley, Salomon Smith Barney, or PaineWebber. Many medium-size and most smaller firms are privately owned. These underwriters contest against each other, technically according to a special set of SEC and MSRB (Municipal Securities Rulemaking Board) rules. But in practice we comply with a much harsher regulator: our perennially ferocious competition. This underwriting process defines the primary market. After bonds are distributed to investors, they enter the *secondary,* or trading, market.

A Public Sale

We have seen how, after a municipality decides to sell bonds at public bidding, its financial people, often assisted by an outside consultant, design a borrowing plan. When the timing seems right, they advertise the issue, inviting interested parties to submit sealed bids, at a specific time and place. Municipal bond dealers submit nearly all proposals, with five bids per issue something like an average.

Syndicate Letter—Participations

Undivided Account

$50,000,000 Milwaukee County, Wisconsin
Selling 12:00 EDT, April 7, 1999

MEMBERS AND PARTICIPATIONS

Manager A	$20,000,000
Manager B	10,000,000
Major A	5,000,000
Major B	5,000,000
Major C	5,000,000
Member A	2,000,000
Member B	1,000,000
Member C	1,000,000
Member D	1,000,000
	$50,000,000

Please call in your pricing ideas to 212-722-8446 before 4:00 P.M. EDT, April 6, 1999

Figure 7

The Bidding Process

Bids usually come from dealer *syndicates,* which pool their marketing knowledge, share the risk of owning an issue, and contribute sales power. Each group is led by one *lead manager* who *runs the books,* that is, sets up the account, holds meetings, and makes many other account decisions. When managers see a competitive sale announced they line up their syndicates (on larger deals averaging about ten members), often basing membership on the last public sale of this bond. Competitive syndicates may also list comanagers, majors, and just plain members, each bracket arranged according to participation such as shown in Figure 7.

Undivided Accounts

The participation percentages determine how profits or losses are split. In *undivided accounts* (sometimes called *Eastern accounts*) each member receives exactly his participation's percentage of the whole issue's underwriting profit. So if the account finally nets $100,000, Manager A, who has $20 million, or 40% of the issue will get a check for $40,000. Member A, who is in for $2 million, or 4%, will get $4,000, and so forth. Naturally, should an account show a loss, bills instead of checks go out, again based on participations.

Note that we're only talking about the underwriting profit, that is the account's gross profit, less all expenses. Not any money made through sales, a completely separate matter. If little Member D had sold half the whole issue by himself, he would get whatever takedowns he earned, but his underwriting check would still have read $2,000.

Similarly, should an undivided account terminate with some bonds unsold, each member is liable for his original underwriting percentage of the remaining bonds. So if despite Member D's heroic sales efforts, should $10 million West Virginias remain unsold in the account, they would receive their share,

$200,000 worth, to dispose of, probably at a loss. We will cover less frequently seen *divided accounts* in Chapter 12.

Syndicate Procedures

Shortly before a sale, each competitive bidding group holds one or more *syndicate meetings* (usually by telephone, but occasionally in person). In these, without knowing the levels competing groups are considering, the members set their bid. The art of underwriting lies in setting interest rates attractive enough to persuade investors to buy but low enough to beat the competing bidders.

At the meetings, discussion focuses on a *scale,* a string of yields assigned to each of an issue's maturity years. As discussed, yields usually rise as maturities lengthen, for instance, from 4.00% for bonds due in one year, 5.00% for those due in five years, out to 6.00% in thirty.

At the hour specified, community officials open the bids, check them for completeness, and then huddle with their financial people to determine whether to accept the best one. Sometimes they reject all bids, usually because they had expected a lower interest cost. But almost always they award the bonds to the winning bid—the one offering to buy the bonds at the lowest interest cost.

NIC and TIC

Since most new issue bidders name several interest rates, along with one dollar price, how is the winner determined? In former years, communities simply totaled the amount of interest to be paid, added any discount or subtracted any premium, and divided this by the bond years, to arrive at a *net interest cost,* or *NIC.* However, NIC ignores the time value of money, so most larger communities now use a more complete formula, *true interest cost,* or *TIC,* to determine the best bid.

While the issuer tabulates the bids, the underwriting

groups check with one another to determine who is high, and the winning syndicate starts offering the bonds at their scale. How is this done? Mostly by telephone, as salesmen call their customers, traders call other dealers and release the scale and concessions over the Bloomberg, Munifacts, Kenny, and other wire systems. These offerings are made on a when issued (W.I.) basis and subject to receiving the award. When the issuer officially confirms the purchase, the manager notifies members, who continue their sales efforts.

When Issued

When issued, or W.I. (technically when, as, and if issued and received by us), means just that—new deals are offered subject to the bonds actually being received as contracted. Once in a long while a legal technicality surfaces after the award and the deal falls through. If that happens, dealers who sold the bonds are released from liability to deliver them, with the legend W.I. having signaled that remote possibility. New issue confirmations are sent without money figures, since the exact settlement date is not known. This W.I. state continues right up to the time when the bonds are actually delivered to the underwriters. If everything goes according to plan, the bonds are duly delivered and paid for. So we see that the life of a competitive new issue has four stages:

1. Before the sale: unborn, so to speak.
2. After the high bidder is known, when the bonds are offered subject to award.
3. After the award has been made, when the bonds are offered W.I.
4. For regular delivery, when the bonds are traded and billed with a fixed settlement date.

Sales Efforts

At sale time, investor enthusiasm comes to a natural peak and customers may place their orders with a syndicate member. The members in turn enter them with the managers during an *order period,* often lasting one hour, during which all orders are treated as entered simultaneously. The manager tabulates them and then chooses which bonds to allot to which members. What happens where there are more orders than bonds? The manager decides.

The Takedown System

When investors buy most securities—stocks, for instance—they pay a certain price *plus* a commission. Municipal bond customers, however, may buy at the advertised scale price, *net,* paying no commission. How does this work? To promote sales, part of a syndicate's gross profit goes into a *takedown* system whereby members take down (buy) bonds from their syndicates at the set scale price, *less* (minus) a concession (a percentage discount).

If you as a salesman persuade a customer to buy $25,000 bonds of a new issue, you hand your underwriting people the order, which they then enter with the syndicate manager. If the manager decides to allot those bonds to your firm and if the underwriter chooses to honor the order, that customer gets the bonds, and you get your commission. However, new issue orders often come in bunches, so don't count too heavily on getting yours filled.

Additional Takedowns

The takedown system provides the incentive and reward for members who sell bonds to retail customers—individuals and smaller institutions. To reward sales to outside dealers who are not members of an account, an *additional takedown* system may apply. If, for instance, the concession is 1/4, there might be an additional takedown of an extra 1/8. So the *total takedown* would be 3/8 of a point. (Sometimes this 3/8 is called just *the takedown,* confusingly.)

This takedown system was an almost universal syndicate practice through the middle 1980s, and is still in effect in many groups, especially for smaller and more local issues. However, competition, particularly the growth of tax-exempt mutual funds, which has consolidated bond buying in fewer and larger hands, has brought many changes. We cover some of these in Chapter 25.

Selling from Syndicate

If enough orders are entered to sell out a whole issue, the bonds are all allotted, the account is closed, and the anticipated underwriting profit is made. However, if after the order period some bonds are unsold, the manager releases a report called the *run and balance,* showing how many bonds remain in which maturities, and the group continues its sales efforts. After the order period, bonds are not subject to allotment. Members just call the manager and take down bonds according to syndicate terms. So if a salesperson gets an order or a trader wants to own the bonds, underwriters simply take them down from the account—first come, first served.

What happens if bonds remain in an account more than a few days? Often investors or dealers will submit bids to the syndicate at prices below their list. Or the group may rethink its commitment and decide to cut the issue price, thus reducing their profit. In especially difficult underwritings they may liquidate the remaining bonds and take a loss. In that case, the bonds are released from syndicate restrictions and enter the secondary market, where they trade according to supply and demand.

Syndicate Bookkeeping

After the bonds are all sold, the account is closed. The manager proceeds to add up the syndicate's profit, subtracts the expenses, completes the bookkeeping, and sends members profit checks (or bills, if there is a loss). MSRB Rule G-12 states that this must be within sixty days after the bonds have been delivered, preventing managers from holding onto profits interminably. Many years ago our annual satiric *Daily Bond Crier,* published by the Municipal Bond Club of New York for its annual outing at the Westchester Country Club, once roasted a West Coast bank underwriter then notorious for sticky fingers. It pictured an exhausted mule team struggling eastward through Death Valley, carrying a heavy load of overdue syndicate checks.

12

Negotiated Underwriting

The other way new issues are underwritten is by *negotiated sale.* In former years, most deals sold competitively—the few negotiated deals came as large initial offerings of semispeculative revenue-backed construction projects. Perhaps the most dramatic of these came in the 1950s, when the New York Thruway and New Jersey, Ohio, and other states' turnpikes were financed this way. We would get all of a new road's financing done at once, see it built, then hope that the revenues would meet debt service. It may now seem strange that a few-hundred-million-dollar issue to build the only good road between New York City and Philadelphia might fail financially. In fact, several of these early issues did very well. However, two just barely survived (Maine and Kansas Turnpikes), and three (West Virginia Turnpike, Chicago Calumet Skyway, and Chesapeake Bay Bridge and Tunnel) fell into deep default.

However, leaving ancient history behind, issuers have come to see the significant advantages of selling certain kinds of deals noncompetitively. So many states have brought their bond-authorizing legislation up-to-date, permitting more negotiated sales.

What factors can give negotiated deals an edge over competitives? (1.) Negotiated managers can shape deals to suit changing investor needs. (2.) They may bargain between buyers more effectively. (3.) Their underwriting risk is often much lower, since most issues are largely preplaced before the sale. (4.) The issue may be timed optimally, at the underwriter's choosing. All these factors tend to lower the cost of financing. And as nothing succeeds like success, in 1998 negotiated deals comprised almost three-quarters of the total new issue volume.

Negotiated Managers

Who does all this negotiating? About ten substantial dealers who regularly negotiate the largest, national-size deals. And another hundred or so who typically manage regional or local deals. They maintain staffs—from two hundred down to a handful of public finance people who actively look for deals and bring them public. What about the other underwriting dealers? If they're lucky, they get invited as plain members to some negotiated parties.

Types of Negotiated Offerings

Negotiated issues come in three layers of complexity: (1.) the first offering of a new issuer, the most difficult to bring; (2.) a subsequent issue of a series already outstanding but containing some new or altered features (these first two types typically apply to revenue bonds); (3.) the latest of a string of well-known, market-tested issues. These last tend to be familiar revenue bonds, or G.O.s, usually presenting the simplest underwriting task.

The Negotiated Landmarks

As with competitive underwriting, negotiated deals have their distinctive high points, but they are more fluid—the issuers and managers set their own pace, without rigid requirements. In preshaped deals, the issuer's finance department begins the task. But when the manager is in on the shaping, they and the issuer start the ball rolling by signing an underwriting contract. In either case, there are five sets of work to tackle: (1.) structure: designing the issue; (2.) credit: dealing with the financial services; (3.) information: communicating with investors; (4.) marketing: syndicating, pricing, and buying; and (5.) sales: distributing, closing, and settling. Each part has its milestone:

the Official Statement, the ratings, meetings with buyers, the offering scale, and the profits.

Structure

What are the basic structuring problems to attack? (1.) creating a bond that investors will buy; (2.) making the issue so strongly backed that it gets good ratings and low insurance premiums, at the same time not overengineering it, for instance, by tying up excessive community income; (3.) obtaining the approval of a respected law firm, affirming that the issue is binding and tax-exempt, as usual; (4.) preparing an O.S.; and (5.) securing agreement between underwriter and issuer on all points. When these matters have been resolved, the issue is fully designed and can proceed to the next stage.

Credit

In issuer-originated deals, sometime during this structuring process a manager has to be chosen. Either overtly or privately, potential underwriters vie with each other by presenting credentials, twisting arms, and using any kind of pressure they can, political or otherwise. Eventually one manager gets the deal, often just before a negotiated issue nears final form. Then either the manager or the issuer applies for a rating to the financial service *rating* agencies for an assessment of the proposed bond's quality. The services maintain a set of guidelines for the various ratings, well understood by the public finance people. There may be considerable interaction between them, especially requests for further information. At the same time, the potential credit enhancers may also study the coming issue. They and the managers may then discuss insuring the bonds and begin to bargain for terms and premiums. When ratings and enhancement are announced, sometimes in preliminary form, the issue can go forward.

Information

After the underwriting contract is signed, the manager mails out "the papers" to potential buyers and dealers, describing the issue in detail. These may include a preliminary O.S. (or *red herring,* as in the color of the front page ink warning that it's not the final prospectus), the legal opinion format, the indenture, and a whole series of economic and other comparisons. In many cases, particularly with large or novel issues, the manager often conducts *information meetings* in several cities to further describe and promote the deal and to respond to investor reactions. Although these are called "dog and pony shows," they may set the tone for the issuance.

Marketing

As sale time approaches, the manager forms the syndicate, usually inviting in some comanagers and sometimes other dealers. Who gets into a specific deal? Normally dealers who have treated this manager well recently. Also, issuers may require inclusion of certain members, especially local dealers. In addition, managers have to consider minority dealer preference status, not to mention keeping peace in the municipal bond industry.

Assuming that satisfactory ratings and insurance have come in, the manager's institutional salespeople now contact large-scale investors, particularly the tax-exempt funds. Here the current needs of these investors can often be met by reshaping maturity amounts and coupons to optimize yields and increase sales. Frequently buyers' bonds are priced not absolutely, as at a 4.65%, but in reference to an outside standards, such as U.S. Treasury bonds, so many basis points lower in yield, tending to protect both underwriter and buyer. The group now *prices* the issue; that is, tests investor response with a provisional scale of interest rates and yields. If demand is too low, the offering yields are adjusted upward; if too high, downward, until a reasonable balance is achieved.

Sales

During this period the group continues to bargain with large buyers until enough orders are in hand to suit the manager. To a certain extent managers share this information with the issuer and then bargain for profit margins and any remaining details. When agreement is reached, the issuer awards the bonds, officially selling them to the syndicate. At that point the manager releases the final scale. Now hundreds of salespeople offer the remaining bonds to their smaller customers, subject to allotment and of course at the fixed price scale. An order period follows, and members enter their orders. Then the manager decides who gets which bonds, allotting perhaps hundreds of millions of dollars' worth, along with their takedown profits, at their discretion. If all goes well, the bonds are completely sold and the syndicate makes its expected profit. If not, the remainder is handled thereafter as in a competitive account.

Divided Accounts

According to legend, a high executive at either First Boston Corp. in New York or John Nuveen in Chicago long ago saw a number of losses his tax-exempt bond department was suffering as manager, even when they had sold more than their share of the bonds. And so he invented the *divided account* system. In these so-called *Western accounts,* bonds that members sell discharge their liability proportionately. In these accounts, heavy sellers (often the managers) automatically chalk up profits and light sellers may later receive their share of any unsold bonds. Divided accounts may be more suitable to issues with large numbers of bonds due in one maturity year, so-called term bonds. In any case, divided accounts are now relatively rare, and using them didn't prevent F.O.B. from closing its municipal doors in 1994.

Modern Takedown Practice

Back in the 1980s, under increasingly fierce competition, large customers started to demand the concession discount and some managers began to give it to them, eroding the price wall between investors and dealers. Then buyers started wanting the takedown as well, leaving the syndicate with only the underwriting spread as profit. Since the largest institutions, chiefly the mutual funds, would place enormous orders, dealers accommodated, and now in larger deals the old takedown system has been replaced by case-by-case, intensively negotiated pricing and awarding. Efficiency has replaced inefficiency, smaller rewards have replaced larger, and smarter and more aggressive underwriters have replaced smaller and less agile ones—better for the funds, about the same for the biggest managers, but much worse for the medium and smaller underwriters, who have dropped like flies. You hear formerly active dealers talking about the old days and how enjoyable underwriting used to be. The remaining underwriters just shrug, maybe thinking that Wall Street's real fun is in making money.

All in all, underwriting, both publicly bid and privately negotiated, is a varied and challenging job offering dealers multiple possibilities for profit and satisfaction.

13

Interest Rates

Supply

Economists tell us that interest is a form of rent, or payment for the use of money over time, quantified as an annual percentage rate (APR). As we saw earlier, in bonds we express this return as yield to maturity—5.00%, 6.35%, and so on. These yields, the interest price of money, go up and down, reflecting the current market levels. You Wall Streeters understand that when the supply of anything rises, its price tends to fall. And of course in bonds that means their yield rises, price and yield moving inversely. In this book bonds are mostly described in dollars, with higher prices meaning *up*. In this chapter, because now we are discussing *interest rates,* we price bonds in yields, where higher yields mean *down* in price—the real world of dollars and cents.

So, when the *supply* of bonds goes up, their interest rates usually rise (as their dollar prices fall). Why? Because at the old yields there are no longer enough buyers to take on the supply. For instance, when we face a heavy calendar—that is, a large future supply of new issue municipals—yields often rise, bringing in more buyers. Perhaps by one .05, as from a 5.50% to a 5.55%, or five basis points. On the other hand, when the calendar is light and bond supply falls off, interest rates tend to fall, as buyers see fewer bonds for sale. This might bring a yield decline of ten basis points, perhaps from a 4.30% to a 4.20%.

In a way, our freely traded bond market resembles traffic in a large city. The issuers and investors represent the multitude of drivers, coming and going as they choose, either crowding or emptying the streets. Traffic lights and stop signs resemble the laws that regulate our flow of money traffic. And who is that waving his arms at the busiest intersection? An informed traffic cop—the Federal Reserve System.

Supply Factors

In addition to the supply of bonds, the amount of money in the economy rises and falls. What factors tend to enlarge the *supply* of money? Increased savings, higher foreign investment levels (often fueled by a cheaper dollar), and expansive moves by the Federal Reserve all tend to increase the U.S. money supply, pushing interest rates *down*. The opposites, lower savings rates and foreign buying and Fed contracting, tend to lower the supply of money, pushing interest rates *up*. Back in 1980 the Fed engineered an extremely dramatic shrinkage of the money supply, draining dollars from the banking system until some short-term taxable rates soared over 20%.

Where can we see the elements affecting interest rates developing? In a number of widely watched and forecast indicators. Every day, in Fed activity in the open market, and weekly, in economic numbers, and also monthly, in the amount of money flowing into various mutual funds, stocks, bond, and money markets.

What factors affect these figures? When banks suddenly offer large amounts of funds, when the Federal Reserve is buying U.S. Treasuries (thus pumping money into the banking system), and with economic developments such as increased rates of personal savings, the money supply is pushed up, relieving downward pressure on interest rates. The reverse of these tends to decrease the supply, pushing rates up.

Federal Funds and Open Market Operations

Commercial banks must maintain a certain percentage of their deposits (in 1999, 3% for smaller banks, 10% for larger) as *required reserves*. Like people with hefty balances in personal checking accounts, banks often end up with more than they need, *excess reserves,* for one or more days at a time. Banks buy and sell these balances between themselves, trading them at the *federal funds rate.* This rate is extremely sensitive to Federal Reserve *open market operations,*—that is, as the Fed changes its holdings of U.S. bonds. Whom does it buy and sell with? The registered government bond dealers, now forty-one strong. When it buys bonds from these dealers credit is eased, because the dealers take the money and deposit it in their banks. The banks then have more money to lend out or invest and also to sell in the funds market, tending to drive bond prices up and yields down. In reverse, when the Fed sells Treasuries, it tightens credit, as money leaves the banking system, pushing up the funds rate. So it's easy to see why we watch the Fed funds rate closely.

The Discount Rate

The Federal Reserve is our *lender of last resort.* So if a bank gets into real trouble it may, with special permission, borrow reserves from the Fed, fortunately a rare event. Also, if at the end of a day a commercial bank suddenly finds that it has insufficient reserves, it may borrow in the funds market. It also has the option of borrowing directly at the Fed's discount window, repaying as soon as its situation straightens out. In both these cases the Federal Reserve stands as our financial backstop.

And in times of market distress, the Fed may plainly announce that it will provide for any legitimate money need. For instance, when the stock market plunged 30 percent in October 1987 the Fed announced that it would lend the banks whatever they needed, as usual at the *discount rate,* the APR, which the Fed charges banks when they need reserves. This discount rate is not a market rate; it's set by the Fed, which changes it only infrequently. Since discount borrowing is relatively small, the rate is less economic and more symbolic, but changes in it usually signal a serious money policy change.

Other Fed Tools

Thus, the Fed may influence interest rates by short-term open market operations and discount rate signals. It may also make a *coupon pass*—that is, buy or sell longer-maturity Treasuries, adding or subtracting bank reserves, often to counteract seasonal factors. Also, the Fed has another and particularly powerful tool—changing banks' reserve requirements. These extra reserves may be lent out many times over, adding or subtracting that much lending power to the banking system. In addition, the Fed sets *margin requirements,* both signaling its attitude about the stock market and changing the credit equation there. Finally, the Fed talks, usually through the chairman and usually by dropping hints. For instance, in December 1996 Greenspan called the stock market rise "unsustainable," and the equity market dropped sharply. Jawboning, it's called.

So the Fed powerfully influences the short-term market, chiefly through the banking system. What about long bonds? How come long bonds, including tax-exempts, usually move with short-term government interest rates? Because dealers and investors pay such close attention to Fed operations, especially tracking its current view of inflation, long bonds' worst enemy.

Inflation

The direct enemy of bond principal is rising interest rates, which automatically bring down bond value. And interest rates are often driven by fears of inflation. Why is this? Well, in 1978, $6,000 bought a standard Chevrolet, while the same amount in 1999 barely buys a snowmobile. Such shrinkage shows what inflation does to hard-earned savings. When bonds come due, their fixed principal can only be spent at the then prevailing prices. And even at relatively low levels, inflation eats up bond purchasing power every year, compounded.

The Real Rate of Return

Let's take the measure of this persistent foe, the indiscriminate attacker of principal and interest, too, and see how to defend your customers, and yourself as well. To do so accurately you're going to have to calculate what the rate of inflation will be in the foreseeable future. As one guide, in the past twenty years the Consumer Price Index has gone up an average of about 3% annually, once reaching 13.5%, though now, in 1999, it's under 2%. See Tax–Exempt Bond Yields versus CPI Changes chart. But even a 7% bond yield doesn't help much when prices are rising at the same pace, so more important to investors is the *real rate of return.* How do we calculate this real, spendable interest rate? *Yield minus inflation.* Which is higher, a 7% yield, or a 5% yield? It depends. A tax-exempt 7% minus 7% inflation gives a zero real return, nothing on your money. But if you can get a 6% yield when inflation is at 3% you have bought a much better deal. 6% minus 3% leaves a real income of 3%.

The managers of the U.S. economy, especially the Federal Reserve, have learned a lot about controlling inflation, but don't count on it too heavily. No one has a reliable crystal ball, and no one can dependably predict future inflation rates. If you believe the inflation rate will go up, beware of long-term bonds, municipal or other. When you can again get a 3% *real* return, then you or your customers will have a better chance of achieving reasonable savings goals.

Demand

Not only does supply affect bond yields, government, corporate, or municipal, but *demand* does, too. This is only natural—when more investors want to buy more bonds, their prices go up and their yields *down.* And when investor demand slacks off, the opposite occurs—prices down, yields *up.* More demand leads to lower rates; less demand, to higher.

What factors usually cause an increased demand for municipal bonds? Expectations of lower yields, increases in savings

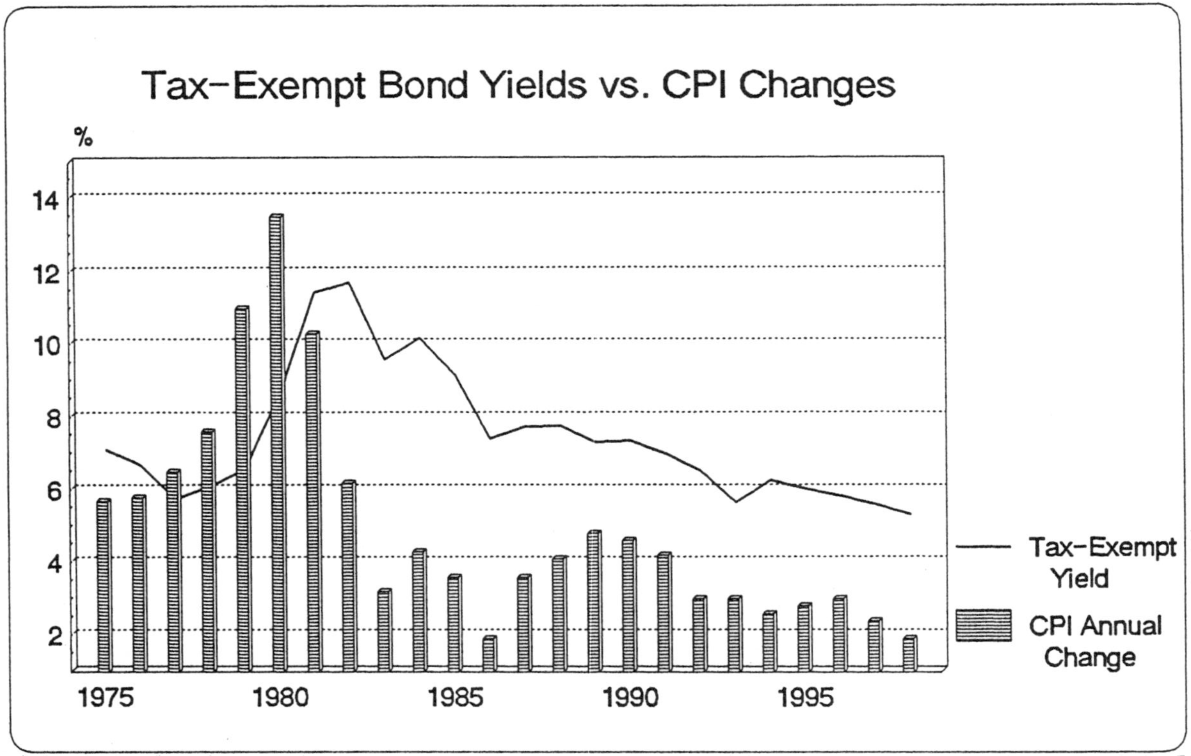
Tax-Exempt Bond Yields vs. CPI Changes
%
14
12
10
8
6
4
2
1975
1980
1985
1990
1995
Tax-Exempt Yield
CPI Annual Change

Figure 8

rates, and higher tax rates, both federal and local. For instance, in 1990, when the economy began to falter, interest rates fell as the Federal Reserve began to pump money into the banks, through open market operations. Many people predicted that bond rates would go down, signaling a time to buy, correctly, as it worked out. Municipal bond yields declined sharply, on long bonds from 6.50% down to 5.25%, and their prices rose by more than ten points.

When the wind blows in the other direction, with expectations of higher rates, decreases in savings, and lower taxes, it tends to push rates *up*. Stronger economic news, such as a sharp decrease in the monthly *unemployment* figure, acts as you would suppose. With fewer people out of work inflation may seem more threatening, bringing the possibility of higher interest rates.

What do you think happens to bonds when, for instance, *employment* levels are announced and instead of rising by an expected 200,000, they have risen by 350,000? Traders and investors see that the economy is robust, eventually creating higher demand for money and increased interest rate levels. If before the news you had been bidding a 5.75% for a thirty-year municipal, what do you think you might be willing to pay after this news? If you guessed a 5.85%, you would be on the right track.

Short, Medium, and Long

We've explored how supply and demand, inflation, and economic factors sway bond yields. How do these intersect? Supply and demand operates most powerfully in the short-term market. Who cares about next year when you're trading bills due in a few months? However, economic news and, with it, inflationary expectations tend to dominate the movements of long-term market yields, especially with governments. Back in the early 1980s we saw an extreme distortion of the usual pattern of yields, when long bonds were yielding 12%, and short ones 15%. At that time, investors were pretty sure that the then-rampant inflation would simmer back down someday, making owning the long bonds at 12% extremely attractive. However, short-term money was very scarce right then, and nearby maturity bonds carried gigantic yields. In between short yields dominated by supply and demand and long-term rates responding to inflation levels come intermediate yields (on five-to-fifteen-year maturities). Their yields usually reflect a blend of short and long factors.

Tax-Exempts versus Taxables

Because U.S. bonds are so actively traded and because in terms of fixed dollars they are principal risk-free, their yields are the standard against which most other domestic bonds are judged. Municipals usually move in the same direction as Treasuries, one up, the other up, and *vice versa.* However, they don't move like riders on a bicycle built for two, always four feet from each other. They are more like two regular bikers traveling the same road together. Taxable U.S. bonds pedal on ahead, yielding more, while their tax-exempt companions trail behind. However, the distances between them vary, with municipals sometimes almost catching up and sometimes falling far behind. We measure this differential by subtracting—Treasury yields minus good grade tax-free yields—producing one form of *yield spread.* The Tax–Exempt versus U.S. Treasury Yields chart shows the powerful correlation. Govvies down, tax-exempts down, but in varying distances.

We often express this relationship in another way, as a percentage. Take the tax-exempt yield and divide it by the Treasury yield in the same maturity. When returns on long-term, good-quality (A-rated) municipal bonds are at least 83% of long Treasuries, their holders usually do well. When, for instance, long U.S. bonds are offered at 7.25%, and you can buy good-grade municipals at a 6.15%, it may be a favorable time to buy them (6.15/7.25 = 85%). Why? Because higher percentages usually come from oversupply for tax-frees, making them relatively good buys. The higher the percentage, the better the deal. If long-term municipal yields rise to 90% of Treasuries, their investors usually come out really well; under 80%, less well; under 75%, they have per-

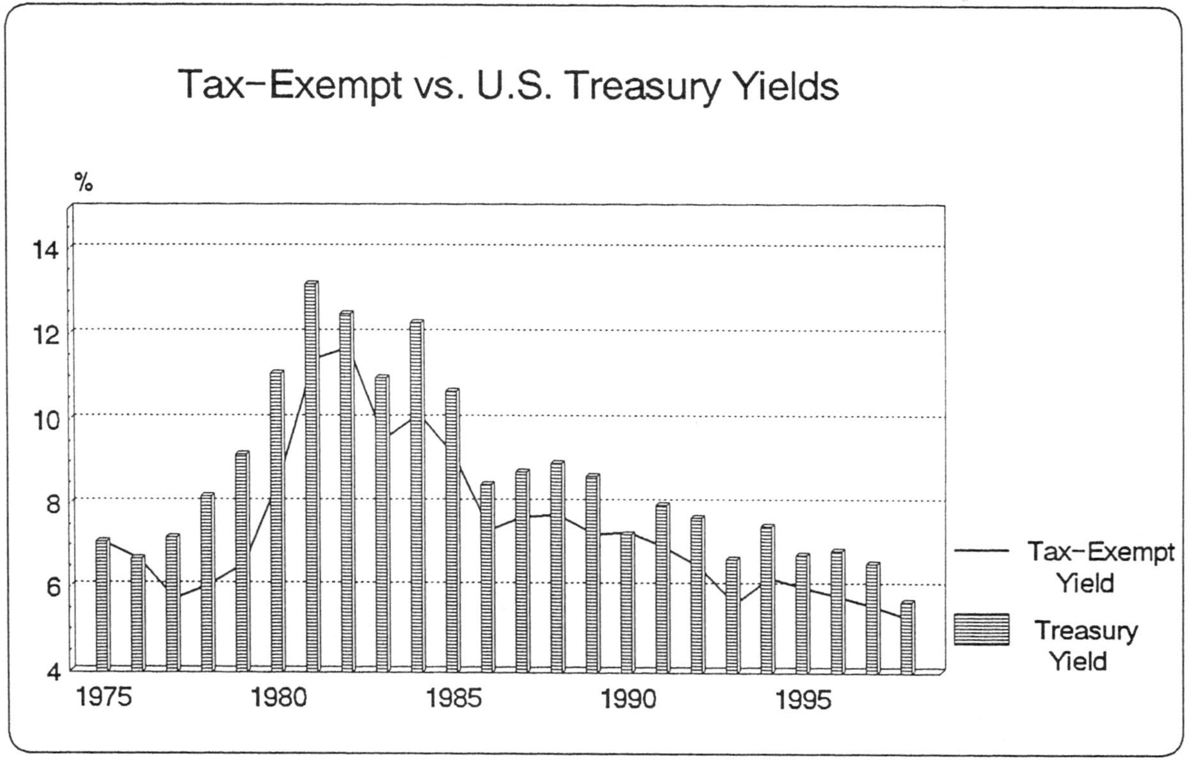
Tax-Exempt vs. U.S. Treasury Yields
%
14
12
10
8
6
4
1975
1980
1985
1990
1995
Tax-Exempt Yield
Treasury Yield

Figure 9

formed poorly. What tax-exempt yield gauge is the handiest to use for this? The *Bond Buyer* index, which appears in most financially oriented newspapers.

What about shorter-term bonds? Most often the shorter the maturity, the lower this percentage, until tax-exempt yields nearly hit the after-tax rate. Why is this? Because the supply of governments is heaviest on the short end, just where it's lightest in municipals.

The Yield Curve

Here we come to a fundamental fact of bond life—*the yield curve.* We've talked a little about how yields normally rise as maturity lengthens—perhaps from a 4.00%, to a 5.50%, out to a 6.00%. Short-dated bonds usually pay the lowest available interest rates, medium-term bonds carry higher rates, and longest bonds still higher, producing an *upward-sloping, positive yield curve,* our most usual bond market pattern. More years, more yield.

Why does the yield curve usually slope upward with maturity? Supply and demand. Most municipal new issues are long-term, and also more people usually prefer short bonds. So both supply and demand drive short-term yields down. Why do people like short-terms? Because they carry less market risk. We saw how new issue scales reveal the yield curve. Also, short-maturity funds typically yield less and are less volatile than intermediate-maturity funds, which in turn yield less and fluctuate less than long-terms. In tax-exempts, maturity and volatility are nearly identical, following the value of the .05.

Liquidity

While we're at it, let's get two terms straight—*liquidity* and *volatility. Liquidity* means how quickly you can sell something and at what expense. How do we measure the extent of liquidity? By the spread between the bid and offered sides of a market. For instance, you can sell $100,000 long-term U.S. bonds any business day and get your money the next, with a tiny selling cost, something like $125. Highly liquid. The market at that time might have been 98 20/32 bid and 98 24/32 offered, just 4/32, between bid and asked.

On the other hand, the same amount of long-term tax-exempts might cost $1,000 to sell. Not nearly as liquid. If a tax-exempt market is 96 bid and 97 offered ("ninety-six–seven"), the one-point spread would have amounted to $1,000. (All of these are calculated before any commissions, which are another subject.) How about other markets? In buying or selling cars or houses, you'd find that their dealers' liquidity numbers might reach 10 or 20%. We'd like their spread, and they'd like our volume.

Volatility

Volatility is different. It means how much the price of something might go up and down, often in relation to original cost. Which are more volatile, govvies or tax-exempts? Since they move in a rough tandem, about the same. On long bonds this converts to a fluctuation of 20%, top to bottom, governments more liquid, both moderately volatile, recently anyway. By the way, here's a good thing to memorize: On long bonds, a shift of 1.00%, or 100 basis points, usually brings roughly a 10-point dollar price change. So the price of a bond whose yield rises 2.00%, say from a 6.00% to an 8.00%, falls about 20 points. And if its yield falls by .50%, its price rises five points, etc.

What about shorter bonds, with ten year maturities, for instance? In recent years they have fluctuated within about the same range as longer-maturity bonds, something like 2.00%. However, as you might expect, their volatility is lower. A 1.00% rise or fall brings about half of the price shift, about five points. And on a one-year bond, 100 basis points is only 1 point, or ten dollars a bond, reflecting the lower volatility of short-dated securities. What's the rule of thumb for a one-year bond? The .05 is fifty cents, and so twenty of them work out to the $10, or one point.

In Practice

How do the concepts of liquidity and volatility affect our ordinary course of tax-exempt dealer dealings? In a number of ways: how dealers set up their *operations;* filling *customer requirements;* and, *speculating.*

Most larger dealers establish a number of different desks—groups of traders and salespeople who work together on a specialty. These desks are often arranged according to length of maturity. So there may be a note desk and short-, intermediate-, and long-term desks, each handling their own range of maturities, and customers. Investors will often have specific maturity needs. For instance, many tax-exempt mutual funds invest solely in short- or intermediate-term bonds. Also, specific customers may have a one-time requirement. If someone had a tax obligation due in the following April, it would be reckless to buy long-term bonds, which might decline in value by the time the IRS bill was due. On the other hand, if the market levels look right to maximum yield buyers, it would be silly not to suggest some long-term tax-exempts. Last, when dealers or investors decide to gamble on a change of interest rates, all things being equal, they most often choose to buy (or sell) long-term bonds, seeking the greatest volatility.

Quality Spreads

You might think that high-, medium-, and lower-grade municipals sell in a similar relationship to each other over a long period of time. For instance, that A-rated bonds sell at 50 basis points higher yield than insured bonds, and so forth. In recent years this has been largely true, but it is definitely not a permanent thing. Supply and demand play a part, so that when a large number of one type of new issue (for instance insured bonds) floods the market, their yields tend to rise closer to uninsured yields.

However, a much more serious determinant is the quality factor. When a particular state or region experiences credit deterioration, such as New York in the middle 1970s, Texas in the late 1980s, and California in the early 1990s, then their medium- and lower-grade bonds tend to fall far away from their high-grades. For instance, back in 1977, after passage of Massachusetts's tax-cap legislation, you could buy good local bonds at 15% yields, extraordinarily cheaper than similar bonds in adjoining states.

Municipal Bond Futures

Speaking of speculation, as with many other financial instruments, the last ten years have seen a tremendous growth in tax-exempt derivatives. What is a derivative? Not a security itself, but an invented takeoff of one, which goes up and down like the security itself, but often presenting more speculative characteristics. In equities, instead of buying all 500 of the S&P stocks, you can buy an index based on it. And in municipals, instead of buying $10 million bonds, dealers and substantial investors can buy *futures* that will move with the *Bond Buyer* tax-exempt index. So for perhaps $100,000 or 1%, they can profit or lose as much as they would have on $10 million bonds.

Dealers use the futures to outright speculate, getting more bang for the buck. They also use them to try to hedge, or protect, their municipal positions. Suppose an underwriter commits to buy a $50 million negotiated deal before he can sell it all. He may decide to short tax-exempt futures to the extent of his unsold liability, locking in his potential profit. Finally, extending this derivative one step, if a trader thinks that municipal yields will change in relationship to governments, he may decide to play the MOB (municipals over bond) spread. In this way a position is taken simultaneously in futures of both municipals and Treasuries. If the trader thinks municipal yields will move closer to govvies, he shorts the Treasury futures and goes long the tax-exempt. This way he makes a profit no matter where the bond market as a whole moves, providing he is right about his gamble that tax-exempts approach closer to Treasuries. And vice versa, should he speculate the other way around.

Part Four

The Secondary Market

14

Secondary Market Overview

New Issues and Old

If all the information you got about the municipal market was from business-directed newspapers, you'd think that it consists entirely of new issues. Beginning life with either a dramatic bidding duel or a newsworthy negotiated offering, they do make easy reading. A new issue's cycle is like a farm's—starting with a syndicate's planning period, proceeding to the offering and sales, and ending with its harvest of profit or loss. Even our trade paper, *The Bond Buyer,* devotes about 99% of its space to the primary market.

But that's only one part of it. Dramatic as new issues are, they usually provide less than half of the municipal bond transaction volume. The rest comes in the secondary, or trading, market where sales routinely top a billion dollars per working day. A bond's primary market phase usually is short—lasting only a few days. But for the rest of its twenty-or-so-year life a bond can trade only in the secondary market.

In a way, the secondary is harder to understand. We have hundreds and hundreds of traders, salespersons, and brokers, calling both each other and thousands of customers all day long, with little reported (the MSRB does issue some trading results and in 1999 is working on more) and nothing like a ticker tape. The secondary is more like a city than a farm—crowded, fast-moving, and loaded with variety. To some it's a jungle.

The Trading Market

There is no Municipal Bond Trading Exchange—our hundreds of thousands of bond descriptions defy such organization. Instead, the secondary market is conducted over-the-counter—in trader-to-trader, over-the-telephone contacts. It operates through an informal network of the same dealers we described earlier, in all states, but firmly centered in New York. Most larger municipal bond firms, and many smaller ones as well, maintain active trading departments.

A secondary market transaction typically begins when an investor tells a salesperson that he or she wishes to sell a bond. The salesperson contacts the trading department and finds what price to pay the customer. If the price is agreeable, the firm pays the customer cash and takes the risk of reselling the bonds at a higher price. The trader may release (offer) the bonds to the firms' sales force in hopes of finding an in-house buyer. Or she may offer them to other dealers, wholesale. If one of these sales techniques clicks, the trader and the house book a profit. If not, they may take a loss.

So the only place investors can get liquidity is in the secondary. Without it, investors would have to hold bonds to maturity, making owning them far less attractive and raising issuing costs. So the secondary market ties directly back to the primary, lowering the cost of community borrowing. In addition, the secondary market provides investors wider varieties of bonds to buy. San Antonio, Texas, might sell a new G.O. issue only twice a year, but almost any day you can buy some San Antones in the secondary.

Three Reasons for Liquidating

Why do people ever sell their nice, safe, tax-exempt municipal bonds? For three principal reasons: Number one: Their personal *financial situation* has changed. Municipals aren't for everyone, or for every year, either, as bondholders adjust their investment strategies. An investor may suddenly find himself in a low income bracket, where municipals make little sense. Or he may need the cash. In the case of a bank or insurance company, it may decide to switch out of tax-exempts and into other securities.

Number two: The *market value* of their bonds has changed. Bond market values fluctuate, sometimes with amazing speed, at other times extremely slowly. I remember once showing my young trading associates a chart of the bond market way back in the sixties and how it had moved only three points in two years. But on that day alone bond prices had shot up three points and then fell five, ending down two, traveling a distance of eight points in a few hours.

Spectacularly or no, municipal bond prices do shift around a lot, creating opportunities for their holders. Traders can buy from a seller, on the bid side, then sell to a new buyer, taking a nice profit. Investors can sell an unfortunate position at a loss, in order to gain a substantial tax break. I've seen investors dump bonds at huge losses, write them off, then swap back into other bonds and ride them up over par, turning a sickening loss into a healthy profit.

The passage of time itself brings shifts. Suppose that fifteen years ago a customer had bought a twenty-year bond; now it will come due in five years. Since short bonds usually sell at lower yields than longer ones, the customer may be able to sell the five-year bonds, reinvest the proceeds in long terms, and substantially increase his or her take-home pay.

Number three: The *credit quality* of a bond changes, sometimes falling, but also often rising. In the last forty years we have seen many urban regions deteriorate and lose favor among investors. The bonds of Buffalo, New York; St. Louis, Missouri; and Kansas City, Kansas, which once brought top prices, later sold at much lower levels. Investors nervous about certain bonds may decide to get out of them before it's too late. On the other hand, holders who buy bonds cheaply, when they are out of favor, may later decide to sell them at good prices and look for other bargains. Also, investors who buy bonds when interest rates are high may see them refinanced, thus creating sale and replacement possibilities.

When, for any of these or other reasons investors want to sell, they have to come to the secondary market. Like used cars, used bonds can be either traded in for new ones or sold outright. One difference, however—investors can't sell bonds themselves; they have to go through a registered expert: a municipal bond dealer.

The Five Trading Parties

So a typical secondary market operation begins with three parties: the customer-seller, the salesperson who handles him, and the house (represented by a trader). It finishes with two other parties: a second salesperson and a new customer-buyer. Sometimes sales and trading are merged into one person, and in other cases more traders, often from outside firms, get into the picture. But five parties make up the most usual trade—two customers and three dealer employees, each party market-compensated.

Taking Risks and Taking Orders

We just described how a trader buys a bond without knowing exactly where he will sell it. The other way traders buy bonds is by *getting an order,* typically on larger blocks, say of over $250,000 worth. This way a dealer finds a customer willing to take the bonds, then buys them from the seller, filling the order without risk.

The Four Trading Classes of Bonds

With all the tax-exempts floating around, firms organize them into four manageable categories, called *desks.* So a larger firm may have a general market desk, an active desk, one for local credits, and one for specialties.

General market bonds bear the larger and better known

names, like G.O.s of Mississippi or Portland, Oregon, or the serial revenue bonds of Chicago's O'Hare Airport. They come in many thousands of different coupons and due dates and generally trade in yield to maturity. On one day a general market desk might be offering $1 million California 5s due 7/1/08 but after they're sold this exact bond might not trade for a long time—like a particular piece of suburban real estate which might resell only infrequently.

The *actives,* or *dollar bonds* originate as a single coupon and maturity from large new issues. They may trade either in yield or in dollar prices, so that we may quote them at 5.04%—5.00% (5.04% bid–5.00% offered), or at 99-1/4 (99 bid, 99-1/4 offered). They often trade busily, for months or years, and are closely watched on Wall Street broker screens. More like apartments in a city condominium building, turning over regularly.

Many *local* bonds tend to trade according to particular circumstances, especially the varying levels of state income taxes. New York, Massachusetts, and Connecticut are currently prominent in this respect, and so many houses assign them to particular state desks.

The fourth category, *specialty* or *high yield* bonds, covers anything that doesn't fit into the others—low-grade, obscure, in default, etc. My kind of bonds.

The Traders

At each desk *block* and *retail* traders sit near one another. The goal of both kinds is the usual—to make as much money as possible in the shortest possible time. However, Wall Street's ferocious competition limits achieving this grand goal.

Block, or institutional, traders deal with larger and professional customers, such as banks, insurance companies, or fund managers. All day long these traders work with salespeople who sit nearby, going long, going short, and soliciting and filling orders. They may also deal in the wholesale market, watching and waiting for profit opportunities, alone and jointly with other dealers. Block trading may be purely speculative or may support new issue operations, among many other functions. An average trade might be half a million bonds, $500,000 worth.

Block traders are notoriously volatile. One morning they may own a huge quantity of bonds and that afternoon none at all, depending on how they like the market. The smaller firms might inventory less than $5 million at a time. Medium sized firms may position $25 million and larger ones hundreds of millions.

Retail traders service a dealer's smaller customers, mostly individuals. They, too, buy at wholesale, and also from the sales force's customers. Since smaller lots of bonds tend to be less volatile than large ones, retail traders operate more steadily than the block guys. They try to keep a level of inventory appropriate for their hundreds or thousands of salespeople to push, owning maybe one week's usual sales volume at any one time. Since neither salespeople nor individual customers can be expected to know their way around the current secondary market, retail traders and their supervisors have an obligation to price bonds equitably. So customers, salespeople, and the house all get a reasonably fair deal. When traders function correctly, chances are that they and the house will be well rewarded.

Sometimes traders, particularly block traders, are viewed as gamblers or even parasites on legitimate investors and sometimes as bumbling idiots, losing pots of money and never knowing when to quit. At other times they seem to take an inspired stand, bringing a whole department fine profits in perilous times. In plain fact, traders do live a rich, full life—some days heroes, some days villains. Trading is a difficult, demanding, and wonderful way to make a living, especially when things are going well. And when the going gets tough, we really earn our keep. Imagine being long $10 million bonds when the market's down five points, and you'll see what I mean.

15

How Traders Buy Bonds

Now I'd like to introduce an imaginary full-service dealer firm, Hudson & West, Inc., and take you to its municipal trading floor. About seventy people work here, buying and selling bonds in the secondary market, with both customers and other dealers. Hudson & West maintains four separate trading desks corresponding to the classes of bonds we talked about in the preceding chapter. Let's see how each of them go about buying bonds.

The General Market Desk

At the near end of the first desk, devoted to trading general market bonds, sit four block traders, headed by a manager. Behind them are the department's dozen institutional salespeople. On the other side of the general market desk are six retail traders. Four assistants, who record transactions, keep track of inventory positions, and work with the liaison people, complete the general market team.

The Active Desk

Next comes the active desk, where on one side three block traders deal in term bonds. They spend all day watching broker screens, making their own markets, and also buying and selling against orders. Three retail traders sit on the other side, along with four assistants, handling smaller lots of actives. This and other desks issue quotes, make bids, and propose swaps all day long. But mostly in vain, since only about a quarter of their efforts result in a trade.

The Local and Specialty Desks

Farther down comes the New York desk, Hudson's local operation. Here sit three block traders, three retail traders, and four assistants. The firm's New York customers, saddled with high income tax rates and with many state issues to choose among, find these bonds especially attractive. Most large dealers maintain separate trading departments in some of their branch offices, but Hudson & West does it their way, handling all trades from New York. At the end of the trading room comes the specialty desk, with a head trader, four assistants, and two researchers.

The preceding four trading positions are risk-taking trading desks. In addition, the department maintains two satellite centers, which feed information to and from them. At one, the *liaison* desk, headed by Arnie, he and five others link the firm's thirty branches to the trading room. Among other responsibilities, they respond to salespersons' questions about bond offerings, relay quotes and prices, and work on payment and bond delivery problems. At the other, the *broker* desk, four people execute trades with the twenty so of Wall Street's brokers' brokers—specialized firms that arrange trades between dealers for a small commission.

The General Market Desk

As flies on the wall of the trading room, we see the following scene unfold on a typical Monday at around 11:00 A.M. Arnie had finished organizing salespeople's requests for prices on about 150 different lots of tax-exempts. These requests may come from customers idly wondering what their bonds are worth, or from those intending an actual sale. Since their traders don't know which is which, Hudson & West instructs them to make a firm bid for every price request. Better safe than sorry. In any case, two of the assistants had been busy transcribing their descriptions onto slips of yellow paper, one for each item. Arnie then sorted the slips into four piles—general market, active, local and New York, and specialty—before delivering them to the appropriate desks.

Making a Bid

A few minutes later a young trading assistant on the retail side of the general market desk picked up their pile and entered some fifty descriptions into the Bloomberg database. She found their current ratings, call features, and other information pertinent to bidding on the bonds. Then she entered this data onto each slip and finally sorted them into two piles, one for lots of $100,000 and over and one for smaller lots. There's where Hudson & West draws the line—$100,000 and over for the block traders, smaller for the retail desks.

Shortly before noon, Philip, a retail trader for general market bonds east of the Mississippi, looked at his share of the new items, eleven lots in all. He picked up one slip, for $25,000 Decatur, Illinois, parking revenue 5% bonds due 4/1/2003. What was he thinking? Although they didn't sound gilt-edged, he saw that they had been escrowed in U.S. Government securities and were now rated AAA by Standard & Poor's. The amount was small but usable, and their five-year maturity was in good demand from the firm's individual customers. He knew that the branches would certainly like these and planned to make a good bid.

But what bid to make? Consciously or no, Philip weighed about twenty different pricing factors, including those factors covered in Chapter 13, the level of his inventory, and his recent trading results. Then he got down to brass tacks.

Traders try to organize the multiplicity of tax-exempt bond descriptions by referring to a two-element matrix comprising maturity and credit quality. For instance, the matrix yield of escrowed bonds due in five years, then 2003, centered around a 4.25%. Six-year escroweds carried a yield of a 4.35%, ten years were at 4.75%, out to those due in thirty years at a 5.25%. (Naturally, bonds with other credit rankings have their own, different scales of yields.) Is the current matrix published? Yes, one version, can be found in the set of scales run every day on the Internet at http://www.kennydrake.com. In addition, every trader has his own variant, either written or mental. In fact, this matrix is a serial bond trader's chief working instrument, and Philip knew well that most municipals trade on or near its numbers.

Philip looked at the department's Friday sheets and saw sales of five items similar to these, noting their profits—from $2 to $13 per bond. He also saw that two small lots of other high-grade bonds due in 2003, had traded that morning, both at a yield of 4.30%. Philip thought that these Decatur bonds would be an easy sale a little cheaper, perhaps at a 4.40%, and this would be a little better buy for him. He entered the 4.40% into the department's computer and subtracted the profit margin he had in mind, 1 1/2 points, or $15 per bond, producing a bid of 101.16. That was the price Philip would authorize a salesman to pay his customer.

Philip handed his bid to the head of the retail trading desk. She glanced at it, then looked at their trades. That morning the department had already sold $3 million worth of bonds but so far had bought only $1 million. She handed the slip back and told Philip to get his bidding shoes on. This was her way of saying to be more aggressive on this and other bids. Why bid higher? First, to pay the customer a fair price. Second, to increase their chances of buying the item.

Philip complied—his was not to question why. He raised his bid by ten basis points, now planning to reoffer them at a 4.30%. After subtracting the same $15 per-bond profit margin, this came to a bid of 101.62.

Note that an anticipated profit of $15 per bond was built into this bid. Retail desks don't try to outguess the market—that is left to block trading. This desk tries to buy bonds at saleable levels, less a built-in spread. In the Decatur case, the 4.30% level was well set, and Philip designed a bid to produce a gross profit of $15 a bond, or $375.

Philip then bid on his other items and handed them to the

head trader, who changed one or two slightly. She initialed the bids and put them in the out box, on their way back to the branches where they had originated.

How would Philip's bids to customers have compared to those he was making in competition in the wholesale market? Hudson's instructions were to make the same bids in both, and he followed the rules. Other firms do it differently, some protecting the selling customer with stricter policies, while others take a greedier approach. Notice that Hudson & West is trying to take a risk on the Decaturs. If they buy them, no matter what happens in the market, the firm will take the profit or the loss.

Customer bonds like these are only one source of inventory for municipal bond trading departments. As we will see shortly, traders also spend much of their day entering bids via the broker wires and to other dealers. That wholesale part of the market resembles an auction, where the highest bidder buys the article on the block. For how traders sell their bonds, see the next chapter.

The Active Desk

We discussed actives earlier—coming from large new issues, each term bond bearing just one coupon and one maturity year. At Hudson & West's active desk three block traders were keeping their eyes glued to an array of brokers' screens displaying up-to-the-second markets on a dozen different bonds. For instance, there might appear a line quoting Indianapolis Gas Revenue AMBAC insured 5% bonds due 8/15/2024 at 98 7/8–99—that is showing a Street bid of 98.875 and an offering at 99.00. This is a difference of just $1.25 per $1,000 between bid and offering. In some markets, many secondary issues will be quoted like this, with narrow spreads between bids and offerings. However, in recent years, since buying has gotten so concentrated in a few large hands, these markets have been trading more by negotiation than through close bid-offered quotations.

With no thought of such matters, an institutional salesman came over to Jim, the head dollar trader. The salesman said that one of his customers wanted to sell $3 million Indys at 99, right on the offered side of the quote. It so happened that Jim had been thinking that the market was ready to jump up and he wanted to buy some bonds before it did. He called out, asking the institutional salespeople if they had any customers who would sell any Indys cheaper than that, at 98 7/8, perhaps. After a minute of frantic phone calling, no one could find any. Jim then shouted, "Buy the three million!," directing his salesman to immediately call the customer and buy $3 million at 99, or $2,970,000. A moment later the salesman screamed, "Bought 'em, at 99!". This way of buying is called taking (or lifting) an offering—that is, buying bonds at the offered price, without negotiating.

See the difference between this and the little Decatur trade? There the plan was to buy the bonds, and then try to sell them, making a built-in profit. Buying on the bid side, selling on the offered side. Here the trader bought the bonds hoping that the market would go up. Buying on the old offered side, to sell on his new offered side.

When Jim glanced at his screen again, Indys were flashing, showing a change, to 99–1/8, so that his purchase at 99 now looked good. The quoted bid he saw was what he had paid, and the best competing offering was now at 99 1/8—that is, 1/8, or $1.25 a bond higher than his cost.

What was going on there? Pure speculation. Their head trader had bought these bonds from a managed fund at 99, probably in hopes of reselling them shortly at 99 1/2 or so, for half a point, or $5 per bond profit. He thought that the market was going to go up, and $3 million was an amount that appealed to him. Half a point on $3 million bonds would mean a profit of $15,000 for the department, a goodly amount these days. Naturally the market could go down instead of up, producing a similar, or greater, loss.

The Broker Desk

We looked briefly at Hudson & West's broker desk, where four people relay bids, offerings, and other information to and from the brokers. Instead of assigning local trading responsibilities to out-of-town branches, Hudson gets bid prices for local bonds other than New York via the brokers. Their philosophy is that you can't do everything. Also, the competitive broker process often gets higher bids for their customers when they wish to sell bonds. The broker puts them out for auction, then gives the highest bid price to the broker desk, who relays it out to the originating branch. If the customer accepts the price, then Hudson sells the bonds to the broker and the customer gets cash for his holding. For more on brokers see Chapter 17.

The Local Desk

As we mentioned, H&W maintains a New York desk. Why do many local bonds need such particular attention? First, many high-tax states issue a multitude of types of bonds, requiring a lot of research and market savvy. Second, many state markets tend to move up and down *within the tax-exempt market as a whole.* Like technology stock prices which often move with other stock prices, but sometimes run counter to them. Like this, the prices of bonds in states such as New York, California, or Connecticut will often rise or fall even when the municipal market as a whole is steady. Or they may rise higher or fall lower when the market is changing. Why do they move somewhat independently? Supply and demand acting on high state tax rates.

In any case, let's look over the shoulder of one of the New York boys. He is looking at a seven-line B.W. page among dozens torn off one of the broker's wire system printers. Six New York items and from one Puerto Rico, which because of its universal tax exemption is treated with New York. He talks to another trader, who agrees with him to make routine bids on six of the items, which he does. Then he takes the other one over to the institutional salesmen, reads out the description and tells them to try to get an order at a 5.20%. As he figured, no response, so he was on his own; he would take the risk of owning them without an order. He jotted down a bid, 5.20% less $7, but would wait until just before the time limit to enter it. A few minutes later, lo and behold, one of the salesmen came over with an order for them, right at the 5.20% net. The order was from a large Boston-based tax-exempt fund. *Miracles never cease,* the trader said to himself.

Naturally the salesman had his own ideas of what to bid, and the trader took them into some consideration. He pondered the number, figuring that if this salesman had the order there were probably some other orders out there, too, at the same price. So naturally, he'd have to work for less than $7, his orderless bid. He wouldn't work for $1, as some would, but $5 was too much. He finally decided to bid in yield, a 5.23%, or a spread of $2.75 a bond. He looked over at the salesman, who hadn't had a trade in weeks and was definitely agonizing. The trader entered the bid, at the last second changing it to a 5.229%, to beat out another bid of 5.23%, and mentally kept his fingers crossed.

Specialty Trading

Meanwhile, the veteran specialty trader was looking at something nice. Another dealer had called him with a B.W. for 50 bonds backed by Northern Airline, which pleased him. We say that this is "getting the call." His desk had already run them through the Kenny data base, and now he looked them up in his own voluminous file. General market and local bonds total more than 95% of all tax-exempts. The remainder comprises almost as many separate names, among them these *special situation* bonds. What are special situations? Rarely traded bonds, those with financial troubles or having a wide variety of other features requiring specific knowledge and particular handling.

Northern Airline was in bankruptcy at the time, and these bonds could suffer with it. They might have completely stumped other traders, who might have bid 20 or 25, what we call a "throwaway bid." However, this man knew that the gates and other facilities built with these bonds were located in thriving Washington County Airport and other airlines wanted them badly. So that the bonds, despite their backing, and their low 4.10% coupon and long maturity, were worth almost 80 cents on the dollar. Easy for this desk, since they had done their homework. In fact, he saw B.W.'s for this exact bond about once a month and bought the majority of them.

Sometimes his desk had to do original research on a new item, such as a rarely traded multifamily housing project. But with the Northern bonds, the trader just checked the last transactions, saw that the research was fresh, and wrote down his bid, 78 1/2. He gave it to an assistant to call in, hoping he would buy the bonds. Less than one bid out of four made to other dealers results in trades, but that's a fact of bond life.

That day Hudson & West's block traders bought six lots of bonds totaling $7 million, going long $4 million and executing orders for another $3 million. The dollar bond boys bought twenty-five lots, $6 million in all. The retail traders accumulated seventy items, forty from the system and thirty from the broker wires and other dealers. The grand total of purchases was 101 different lots with a face amount of $15 million, about an average day for this department. Thus Hudson & West's share of the whole secondary market was about 2% of the nationwide total, typical for a medium sized firm. Now let's take a chapter break and see how the four desks fared with their purchases.

16

How Traders Sell Bonds

In the previous chapter we saw how Philip had bid on 25 Decatur escroweds, how Jim on the dollar desk went long $3 million actives, how the New York desk got an order, and how the junk guys bid on 50 Washington Counties. Now let's see how they all made out.

Back to the Retail Desk

At Hudson & West, small-lot bids were ordinarily good through the day, so salesmen can use them through 5:00 P.M., New York time. As you see, there's a time lag in the small-lot municipal bond secondary market. However, the potential profits are large enough to compensate for it. With blocks it's different—as we will see shortly, their prices may change at the drop of a hat.

At around four o'clock, one of Arnie's Army dropped twelve buy slips in Philip's in box. Among them was one for the 25 Decaturs, meaning that the bonds had been bought from the branch office customer. Before Philip started releasing these buys for the next morning's offering sheet, he rethought the situation. The government quotes were down a bit, but the municipal market was in good overall shape. His bonds were selling briskly, and he noted that the retail inventory position totaled only $5 million bonds. Their limit was $15 million, so there was plenty of room. His feelings on the market were constructive—it didn't seem too high and it was fairly active. What do these factors add up to? A relatively stable, brighter than average trading background.

Other kinds of markets have to be dealt with differently. When prices are falling, retail traders, while keeping some bonds for their branches to work on, periodically mark down their prices, promoting sales before the market goes lower. In strong and rising markets, the challenge is to buy enough bonds to keep up with sales. Had the market shifted sharply or his inventory position changed drastically, Philip might have made adjustments.

Trading Procedures

Like most firms, Hudson & West pays salespeople to buy bonds. So Philip jotted down a $5 per bond gross buy commission on the Decatur buy slip and put it in the out box. How much for the buying salesman? $125, or about $40 net. Philip then took the pink copy of the twelve slips and marked them with the reoffering prices for the Hudson & West system. On the Decaturs it was 103.12, a yield of 4.30%, which left a gross profit of 1 1/2 points, or $375 total. Then Philip's assistant typed up twelve new position cards, all details entered, and put them in their inventory book. She then added these items to Hudson & West's release sheet—their internal list of bonds for salesmen to sell to customers—with descriptions, ratings, prices, and commissions included. By the next morning copies would go out to the firm's control section, its operations department, the buying salesperson, and the customer.

Most of Hudson's salespeople sold tax-exempts only once in a blue moon. But several dozen would soon look at the Decaturs, no doubt noting the nice commission, of which they would earn about a third, or $125 net. Can a salesman just sell bonds without checking with New York? No. All transactions have to be cleared with the trading desk, making sure the item had not already sold or changed in price. Two such sales a day could bring in $50,000 annually, and if this were added to $100,000 in equity commissions, it would be about average for a wire house salesperson these days.

A Dealer Trade

By noon the next day about twenty-five items had sold from Philip's retail general market position. He had bought fifteen new blocks, bringing his inventory down to $4.5 million. He had one "nibble" on the Decatur bonds, meaning that one of Hudson & West's salespeople had asked if they were still available, but they remained unsold. Items this desk doesn't sell internally the first or second day are usually released "to the Street." So, late that afternoon, Philip instructed an assistant to advertise them on Wednesday's edition of both the Munifax and the Blue List nationwide wire systems, showing the offering to hundreds of municipal bond dealers. Philip set the wholesale price at the same yield of 4.30%, less a 1/4 concession (dealer discount).

Next day, Wednesday, a Chicago dealer telephoned Philip and inquired about the Decatur offering. This call started a new episode in an age-old game—buyer versus seller. While he was getting out the card, making sure the bonds were still available, Philip started playing his part—trying to determine what the other dealer's situation was. Was he just inquiring casually? Maybe. Or was he trying to buy the Decaturs for inventory, to sell later at a higher price? Not too likely. Or did he have a firm order from a customer to buy them? Philip decided that this was the most likely case and that he would work on this presumption. So it would come down to how much commission the dealer would get out of him. Philip quoted the dealer the printed price—a 4.30%, less 1/4 concession.

The other dealer said that he would buy them at the 4.30% all right, but at a bigger concession, less one point ($10 per bond). Traders would say, "He was bidding less a point against an offering of less a quarter." This was 3/4 under Philip's price, or 102.12.

Philip figured that if he sold them at the Chicago firm's bid price, he would make 1/2 point, only $5 a bond. He thought a 4.30% was reasonable enough, and the market was quite firm. And since he did a fair amount of business with this dealer he decided to compromise a bit. He would give a little, but no lower than a 4.30% less three-quarters. But first he gave it one more try—he said he would sell them at less 4.30% less 1/2. We would say that Philip was "countering a less one bid with an offering of less a half." The Chicago trader waited a second, then agreed to the 1/2 concession, and Philip confirmed him the bonds. Bought at 4.30 less 1 1/2, sold at less 1/2, a gross profit of $250. As you see, a better horse trader would have bought them from Philip a quarter cheaper.

25M Decatur, IL Parking Rev. 5% 4/1/04
ETM—S&P AAA

S.D. 4/1/99	
First bid	@4.40 = 102.66
Less spread of 1 1/2	1.50
	101.16
Purchase price	@4.30 = 103.12
Less spread of 1 1/2	1.50
	101.62
Retail offering	@4.30 = 103.12
Dealer offering	@4.30 = 103.12
Less 1/4 concession	.25
	102.87
Dealer bid	@4.30 = 103.12
Less 1 concession	1.00
	102.12
Final trade price	@4.30 = 103.12
Less 1/2 concession	.50
	102.62
Purchase price	101.62
Gross profit	1.00

Figure 10

Philip then repeated the whole transaction, amount, description, CUSIP number, coupon, maturity, escrow feature, and the yield and concession, making sure both sides agreed on the trade's terms. At what price did the Chicago dealer sell them? That was his private business. But if his order was at a 4.30%, then his firm would make the 1/2 point concession, a total of

$125. He also might have sold them at a higher or lower price or possibly taken them for inventory, Philip would never know. So here is one of the five-handed secondary market trades we talked about earlier. The selling customer, a salesperson, a dealer, another dealer, and the new buying customer. Philip was satisfied, knowing that the better he handled his trading position, the better his future. Such a trader makes about $75,000 these days and perhaps a three or even six months' bonus if all goes well during a year.

Philip marked the card and handed it to his assistant to check and process. Later, along with all the other sale tickets, it would be taken to the back office. There the trade's exact dollar figure, including accrued interest, would be calculated for settlement three business days later and entered into the firm's and the other dealer's systems. Their confirmations would be electronically exchanged that night through NSCC, making sure both parties agreed. There are about a dozen separate steps in the operations cycle, some performed by hand and others by computer, adding up to substantial expenses.

How did Hudson come out on this trade? From the $250 gross profit the buying rep was paid $40, leaving $210. If you figure $50 in direct expense per trade and another $60 in indirect expense, including something for the trading department, that leaves around $100 for Hudson & West and its shareholders, before tax. Certainly not a way to get rich quick.

Dollar Bond Action

In the last chapter we left the dollar guys looking at a shiny new purchase—$3 million bought at 99, with the market up a bit at 99 1/8. Trader Jim shouted out to his institutional sales force, "OK, gang. One million Indys to go at 99 1/4—that's a 5.05%, cheapest thing out there!" No response. *As usual,* thought the trader. An hour went by and nothing happened. Three of the salespeople said they were going out for a rinse. *Liquid lunch,* thought the trader, washing down his ground-up tuna salad with a diet cola. Then it hit—Govvies down ten ticks (10/32, or 2 basis points), on fresh news. Housing starts were up 4%, not the expected 2%. Immediately the trader decided to liquidate this position and shouted, "We're still long the $3 million Indians—to go now at 99, *CHEAP!*" The remaining salespeople barely stirred, no doubt thinking that if they couldn't sell them before the news, how could they after, even at 1/4 lower? The screen flashed, showing the change at 98 3/4–9.

We use *long* in two ways. One way means bonds of distant maturity dates, perhaps twenty or more years out. Jim was using the other meaning, which means buying or owning a block of bonds. "Going short," a much rarer municipal technique, means selling bonds you don't yet own, in hopes of profiting by buying back exactly the same bonds later, but at a lower price. However, remember the old Wall Street lines:

> He who sells what isn't his'un
> Buys it back or goes to prison.

For the rest of the afternoon the government market drifted down, followed closely by tax-exempts, sending them slightly lower. Just before five, a broker who specialized in dollars called Jim and asked how he was doing Indians. In our jargon the broker was asking for Jim's market on what he was willing to pay and how he was willing to offer these bonds. Jim said, "Eight and a half—nine." He would buy some at 98 1/2 and he would sell some at 99. No amounts were mentioned, but the current trade understanding was at least $250,000 bonds.

The broker said, "I think I might get 3/4 for a couple—can you handle that size?" What did this mean? (1.) That the broker was in touch with a dealer who was interested in buying $2 million possibly at 98 3/4. And (2.) Would Hudson sell that many at that price? Jim replied, "I'd sell two, maybe three, at the three quarters." He was offering $2 or possibly $3 million at a price of 98 3/4. "I'll get right back, Jim. Thanks."

A few minutes later the broker called back. "Jim, I can pay three-quarters for three mil. OK?" Now the price was a definite 98 3/4, and the amount was up to $3 million, his whole block. Jim had no doubts. "You own 'em. Selling you three million Indians at 98 3/4. Done."

"OK, we buy, and thanks, Jim." Then he shouted out, "The Indys are all gone!"

"What price?" asked one of the salespeople.

"At three-quarters, but keep it to yourself, Sally!" But he bet that within ten minutes the whole Street would know about the trade.

So a quick quarter down, or $2.50 on $3 million bonds, a loss of . . . what? Seven hundred and fifty dollars? No! Seventy-five hundred dollars. Why did he sell so soon, below his cost? He figured he had made a mistake, and remembering the old adage, "your first loss is your best loss," he took his lumps and, we can hope, went on to better things.

At the New York Desk

We left the New York desk Monday morning, with the salesman with the order waiting anxiously to hear if they bought the bonds. In fifteen minutes, right at the time limit, the broker called back and sold Hudson & West the bonds at a 5.229%. The broker had seven other bids ranging from 5.35% up to a 5.24%, giving him a cover of $1.45 a bond, not bad. He shouted out to the salesman, "You got 'em! Go sell 'em at the five-twenty." The salesman's face asked two questions: what was his commission, and what was the cover bid? The trader shouted again, "Two seventy-five for you, cover an eighth." The salesman confirmed the bonds, closing out that position. Three days later the broker would deliver them, and Hudson would redeliver them to the customer, grossing $8,000, from which the salesman got $3,300. Not a bad trade.

Specialties Again

At the high yield desk a young second-in-command picked up the phone and bought the 50 Washington Counties from the outside dealer, direct, with no broker in between. She wrote up a ticket buying the bonds at 78 1/2. Then she thought about a possible release price, much as Philip had on the Decaturs.

As mentioned, the source of payments for these bonds, Northern Airlines, was in Chapter 11, voluntary bankruptcy. However, she knew that Northern would probably continue to make the modest payments necessary to pay off these bonds. In addition, about 10% of this issue was scheduled for early retirement every year, through a sinking fund. So, although the bonds were rated CCC (Speculative) by the services because of their Northern name, they were in fact adequately secured. At 81 1/4 they would yield 6.25% to maturity, and more to their expected average life. This represented excellent value, and she released them at that price. She put down 2 points as a sales credit, fatter than on most other offerings, thus also making them particularly attractive to the sales force.

Soon a salesman called the junk desk and *took the bonds firm.* This means that he secured the exclusive right to sell them for one hour. He soon returned with an order, and the trade was done. $1,375 gross profit, of which $1,000 went to the sales department ($350 to the salesman) and $375 was credited to the junk desk. The assistant closed out that card, at the bottom writing $375. This profit brought the junk department's day total to $6,000 and the month's to $90,000. A good start to the new year and another nice bonus. An apprentice specialty trader may now earn $75,000 and, in a good year, three or six months, or larger, bonus on her way up.

Of the $15 million bonds that Hudson's four desks went long on Monday, about one-quarter were sold during Tuesday—$3 million worth through their branch system and another $1 million to other dealers. On these, the firm made a gross profit of about $40,000, of which about $10,000 went to the sales force. In addition, they also sold $2 million bonds bought previously, making $20,000 on them. They had started Tuesday with a total position of $30 million, sold $5 million, and added another $7 million, thus ending the day at $32 million, and were off to a reasonably good month.

17

The Brokers

Glancing back up the trail we've followed so far, we saw how the municipal bond primary market helps finance the construction of public works—the highways, bridges, water and sewer projects, schools, and other community facilities we often take for granted. Now, here in the secondary phase, we are seeing how dealers provide liquidity to existing bondholders and opportunities to new ones. Doing so, they operate in national and regional marketplaces, trading bonds of thousands of issuing communities, and dealing in more than a million separate bond descriptions. No dealer can hope to cover this entire market alone. Enter the *brokers.*

We've already run into brokers (the regulators call them brokers' brokers or municipal securities brokers) several times. And if they seem to pop up all over the place, that's part of their job. What is a municipal bond broker? In short, a middleman. How do brokers operate?

1. They do not own bonds or take risks.
2. They arrange bond purchases and sales, confidentially.
3. They trade only between dealers, not with investors.

As you see, these limiting characteristics clearly define brokers as brokers, different from dealers, who routinely own bonds and take risks and sell to many different kinds of investors. While we're at it, let's check the jargon. We call municipal bond firms *dealers,* and dealers employ *traders,* people who buy and sell bonds in the secondary market. *Brokerage firms* employ individual *brokers,* who arrange purchases and sales between dealers.

How do brokers go about this business? By keeping in touch with as large a universe of dealers and their bonds as possible, by monitoring closely traded markets, and by providing services. Along these lines, a broker tries to bring together the trader willing to pay the highest price on a certain block of bonds with the one willing to sell at the lowest. If successful, the broker earns a commission, averaging about .1 percent, just $1 per bond.

Again, brokers do not own bonds themselves. They act as go-betweens, risklessly. On extremely rare occasions one dealer party to a brokered transaction fails to perform as expected. Then, the other dealer may volunteer to take all, or a part of, any resulting loss. Thus, while dealers may show either a profit or a loss, every broker's trade brings in a commission.

Confidentiality

Following long-established industry practice (embodied in MSRB Rule G-24), the relationship between a dealer and a broker is *confidential.* The identity of the buying and selling parties is not revealed to anyone outside the brokerage firm—before, during, or after the trade. This maintains the privacy of both sides. So the buyer and the seller never talk to each other directly. All communications come only through the brokerage house.

Dealers Only

Brokers trade only with dealers, not with investors of any kind. Why? Their function is to serve their dealer customers, not compete with them.

Accuracy and Integrity

Municipal bond brokers buy and sell verbally, over the telephone, often involving large amounts of money. Since neither dealer party knows the identity of the other, they must rely heavily on both the middleman's *accuracy* and *integrity.* In general, brokers' accuracy is of a high order—there's an old Wall Streetism: "The broker is always right." After all, the broker has the valuable cross-check of seeing both the buy and sell sides of a trade, while dealers have only their own.

As to integrity, some brokerage firms have for many years staunchly striven to earn and defend their reputations for trustworthiness. Others may take a more relaxed approach or have not yet had time to develop an outstanding name. In addition, individual brokers develop their own reputations, which usually correlate with that of their firm.

The Brokerage Companies

In 1999, about twenty brokerage firms are operating in the tax-exempt bond market. They employ an average of about fifteen individual brokers, so there are about three hundred now active in our business. They compete with each other on the basis of personal relationship, market knowledge, and price information. But all brokers are not the same. Some only work on offerings and B.W.s, some just trade actives, while others stick to situation trading, each with its own distinctive routines.

Offerings

Formerly, brokers would remind their counterpart traders of the offerings they thought most attractive. Now, in addition to these personal contacts, many brokerage houses print long strings of dealer offerings, all tidily listed on their screen pages, arranged according to state, maturity, and amounts.

Bids Wanted

When a trader wishes to sell a certain block of bonds, he may instruct a brokerage firm to "go B.W." with them—that is, put them up for sale to the highest bidder, at a sealed auction. Both by phone and on their special bid-wanted screens, the broker broadcasts the item's amount, description, and a cut-off time. Up to then dealers may enter bids, competing to buy. After the deadline, the broker collates the bids (usually via a computer-driven program) and transmits them to the originating dealer. Then the trader decides whether or not to hit (accept) the high bid. If not, there is no trade. However, in about half of most cases, the trader finds the bid satisfactory and gives the broker the go-ahead to sell the bonds. The broker next confirms the sale to the high bidder and goes back and buys them from the seller at the same price, subtracting a commission.

What if an investor wants to sell a block of bonds using this process? She must go through a dealer. Suppose she wants to buy something on a broker B.W. screen? Again she has to go through an obliging dealer, paying a small commission.

Active Bond Brokering

As we have seen, when new issues carry large amounts of bonds with one coupon and due in a single year, we call them *term bonds.* If they trade busily, they become known as *actives* (or dollar bonds). Brokers list actives on special screen pages, such as we saw in the two preceding chapters, where they quote the current highest bids and the lowest offerings.

Dollar bond brokers keep track of their markets on a continuous basis, constantly updating their screens, so that their dealer customers can readily see that a broker knows one dealer willing to pay 99 1/4 and another willing to sell at 99 1/2. Sometimes a broker will put together a trade right on quotes like these. More often, trades come after one or more bids and offers, back and forth between the two dealer parties.

Other Broker Trading

Other kinds of broker trades are called *situations.* For example, suppose Dealer X is offering a million Chicago 5s at 99 1/2 and Dealer Y, who doesn't know who owns the bonds, wants to buy them. If the market is rising, Y may instruct the broker to buy the bonds right at 99 1/2. The broker then buys the bonds from X and sells them to Y at 99 1/2, plus a commission. Again, this kind of transaction we call taking an offering, or a *take.* Even if Y knew who X was, he might use a broker, fearing that X would raise the price or even withdraw the offering, if he approached him directly.

In another case, Dealer V may have been unsuccessful in moving half a million Jacksonville, Florida, bonds at 95. If the market is steady, instead of going B.W. (which might result in a bid of no higher than 94), he may ask a broker to find a buyer for them at a price nearer his offering. The broker may then approach one or more dealers he knows are looking for this kind of bond, perhaps finding one who would pay 94 1/4. After several rounds of bids and counteroffers, he may finally arrange a trade buying them at from V at 94 3/8 and selling them to W at 94 1/2. The broker thus moves a block of bonds that the owner wished to sell and provides the new buyer with a chance for a profit, making a commission in the process. Other situation trading often occurs when outside news hits the market. Then brokerage firms provide dealers with fast-breaking market developments, buying and selling millions of bonds within a few minutes.

The Trade Tickets

After a broker trade has been completed, the three parties involved write up four "tickets," one each by both dealers and two by the broker. On the Chicago example trade, the broker would write his buying ticket, #1, at 99 1/2 and his selling ticket, #2, at perhaps 99.585, thus adding on his commission of 85 cents per $1,000 bond. Each of these will match the other side exactly, with a difference between them of $850, thus giving the broker his commission.

When the four tickets have been completed, either by hand but increasingly by keystroke entry, they go to their respective back offices, as detailed earlier. All as mandated by industry practice and NASD and/or MSRB rules.

Market Sectors

Competition between brokers has reached formidable heights, and they now distribute precise and detailed knowledge of fractional segments of our market. These segments include general market bonds, various regions such as New York, California, New England, or the Northwest, as well as junk bonds, and odd lots.

Commission Rates

What commissions do brokers charge? Each set their own, but often subject to negotiation. Formerly most broker trades were done for 1/8, but in 1998 average commission levels ranged from about $1.50 per bond for trades less than $100,000, through 75 cents for $1 million bonds, to even lower for larger blocks.

Broker/Dealer Styles

So dealers take risks while providing investors liquidity. And brokers narrow the spreads between buying and selling. How do individual traders use brokers? Some tend to use just one or two, leaning heavily on their information and even advice. Others spread their business widely and listen to brokers' opinions, but act according to their own lights. Still others ignore any broker advice, even implied, and have more distant relations with them. A good individual broker can work with almost any of the dealer trading styles. As you may be gathering, running a reputable and profitable municipal brokerage firm requires a considerable amount of effort, expense, determination, and good fortune. Along the way, they distribute large amounts of information, both verbally and electronically. We will catch up on some of these methods shortly.

Part Five

The Services

18

Professionals

We've traveled through the primary and the secondary, and now we go to the tertiary, or third, level of the municipal bond market, to its circle of services. First let's look at the *professionals*—the lawyers and accountants, and the financial experts—all of whom serve bond issuers, dealers, and investors. Later in this part we'll move on to the *raters,* the *information providers*, and the *enhancers.*

Lawyers

Bond people and attorneys interact in three chief arenas: when a bond is being designed, when there's a general legal problem, and when someone's in trouble—situations calling for a *bond counsel,* a *corporate lawyer,* or a *securities lawyer.*

Bond Counsel

Hired by communities but often paid from the proceeds of a new issue, *bond counsel* stand between issuer and investor. Their position is objective—assuring both the community that their new issues are legally designed and also the investor that their bonds are valid obligations. In brief, that they conform to state enabling bond legislation.[1] Although some cities regularly shop around for new bond counsel, more typically they cooperate ongoingly. Bond counsel's work begins when an issue is proposed, signaling them to review their state's bonding statutes. After being officially hired, they cooperate with the city's own lawyers and, particularly in negotiated deals, with the underwriters, who usually employ their own *underwriting counsel.* These latter attorneys review an issue's legal status and guard the buying syndicate's interests.

For instance, on a 1997 Jacksonville, Florida, water and sewer revenue issue, the New York bond counsel firm, Orrick, Herrington & Sutliffe LLP, consulted both that city's own lawyers and Smith Barney's underwriters' counsel, Holland & Knight, of Jacksonville. So a city's lawyers may draft the bond issue's authorizing resolutions that the governing body will pass, bond counsel checks these out for completeness and legality, and the underwriter's attorney reviews the whole process. City counsel may then have to shepherd an issue through state court validation procedures, while both they and the underwriters' counsel make sure that the O.S. is being correctly drawn. Meanwhile, bond counsel checks that all the necessary presale steps, including advertising procedures, have been followed, usually taking a minimum of one month, but more often much longer.

Referring to these and other sources, bond counsel then prepares a *preliminary legal opinion.* First it identifies the borrower, the issue, and its purpose. Then it cites the issuing documents they have reviewed, including the enabling laws. Next it opines that the bonds are valid and binding community obligations and describes the payment source, either general obligation or revenue. Then comes a central point—a description of the bond's state and federal income tax status—whether fully tax-exempt, subject to AMT, or taxable.

Along the way most legals state a number of disclaimers. For the state and city, that the bonds are paid strictly from the specified source and no other. For the lawyers themselves, that they have performed no auditing function, and that the legal opinion will not be updated.

When the issue is ready for delivery, bond counsel issues its *final legal opinion,* sees to it that the necessary closing documents are executed, and personally inspects the form of the bonds themselves, whether printed or book entry. After closing, counsel will organize the issue's documentation into a thick bundle, the *Transcript of Proceedings,* sending copies to the city, the underwriters, and the financial consultant, in case a legal question ever arises. At some point bond counsel sends out a bill. (If you think that I have a favorable opinion about lawyers, you are right. I certainly have had my share of dealing with them, and as a whole I have found them ethical and highly effective.)

Corporate and Securities Lawyers

Most municipal bond market participants need a general, corporate-type lawyer to handle routine legal affairs—contracts and their problems, personnel and customer complaints, and the like. Naturally, most larger firms maintain a legal staff, in-house; most smaller firms keep up a relationship with one or more outside lawyers. More serious problems, such as customer disputes, may call for an experienced *securities attorney.* These lawyers usually manage to help settle things through negotiations with lawyers from the opposing side. However, sometimes they may end up in court or, in arbitration. See Part Seven for more on this.

Accountants

Naturally, accountants and auditors enter the picture, calculating and verifying the figures shown to investors. They prepare the issuer's financial statements, including the revenue, expense, and fund balance numbers, and may be asked to check future projections for reasonability. Finally they will certify that the community's financial picture has been represented fairly, in accordance with generally accepted accounting principles (GAAP) and as modified by the Government Finance Officers Association (GFOA) standards.

The Financial Experts

Of course, our elected representatives set community financing policy. But they usually leave it to experts to put their decisions into practice. Who are these experts? Although smaller communities may rely on experienced volunteers, most medium-sized places hire professional financial advisers[2] from the private sector. What do they do? When it comes to bond issues, they design bridges—between political reality and a desirable market instrument. The largest issuers usually maintain their own staffs of experts to do the job. Whatever their size, financial people perform three main functions: represent the community to the investing public, develop capital plans, and implement these through note and bond sales. In between sales they distribute information, including up-to-date figures to the rating services. And they help communities plan over the long range, figuring what facilities a city needs and when it can afford to build them, often as mandated by state law.

In negotiated deals, many bond designing functions are performed by the underwriter. In competitive deals, financial advisers do this work which falls into these categories:

1. Shaping the issue.
2. Preparing an Official Statement.
3. Bringing the issue to market.

In *shaping an issue* financial people may first estimate what the issue's interest cost will be. Then they can discuss the debt service schedule with the city officials, figuring how much they are willing to pay out each year. This may involve a delicate balancing between saving on interest cost by retiring debt rapidly and spreading the principal payments out as far as practical.

The *Official Statement* is the central document in any municipal new issue, supposedly providing all the information an investor needs to understand it. Although the MSRB can't regulate issuers, it can and does require dealers to send a copy of the O.S. to new issue buyers. And in practice, lawyers insist that all sizable issues come with one, hoping to protect its underwriters from future liability. O.S.s contain: a full description of the issuer, the exact nature of the security, all pertinent features of the bonds, historical information about the source of payment, and a description of the issue's legality, including its tax status. Also, general and demographic data, economic figures, and a long list of disclaimers, citing everything that might go wrong with the bonds. Financial consultants often prepare preliminary O.S.s, particularly with first-time security offerings. (As noted, they usually consult with bond counsel along the way.) They then send this *red herring,* along with all the issue documentation, including the authorizing papers, to the rating services, trying to make the best possible pitch for a good ranking.

In competitive deals, late in this process financial experts will select the date they figure the market will best receive their issue, and advertise it for sale, usually in both local newspapers and *The Bond Buyer.* Meanwhile they may prepare work sheets and an official bid form for bidders to enter proposals. When the rating is received, they send out packages of all this information to potential bidders and investors. On the sale date they monitor the bids for validity and, usually, recommend that the community award the bonds to the winning syndicate.

After the sale the issuer prints up the final O.S., with the definitive information—coupons, prices, ratings, and all the rest. Following MSRB Rule G–32, a copy is sent to all buyers by the settlement date. Then the financial consultants work with bond counsel wrapping up the issue, oversee the preparation of the bonds themselves, accept a check from the underwriters, and invest the proceeds until the city needs the money.

Miscellaneous

A number of other service providers are essential to the smooth functioning of the bond market—systems and computer companies and financial printers. Also the clearing agents, chiefly the Depository Trust Company (DTC) and the National Securities Clearing Corporation (NSCC). Both are nationwide clearinghouse organizations run by their member banks and dealers. Based in New York, they receive, pay for, and deliver all kinds of securities, both electronically and physically.

Notes

1. I have covered bond counsel procedures, step-by-step, in my first bond book, *The Municipal Bond Market: Basics* (Jersey City, NJ: The Financial Press). (Copies available—212-722-8446.)
2. A list of financial advisers and also of municipal bond attorneys, along with their latest annual volume rankings, can be found in the semiannual *The Bond Buyer's Municipal Marketplace.*

19

Rating Agencies

Three financial service companies—Moody's Investors Service (the original rating organization), well-regarded Standard & Poor's, and up-and-coming Fitch IBCA, Inc.—now research and grade thousands of municipal and other bonds and rank them according to their credit strength. The various rating definitions can be found in the services' printed manuals.

How does a rating come into being? When a new issue is projected, the issuers' financial people choose among the services, paying a fee to the ones selected. They then send the credit information to the services, each of which divides rating responsibility into groups such as G.O., electric power revenue, housing, etc., or by region. The rating companies assign the issue to one or more specialists, who analyze it in depth. The analysts then make a letter grade recommendation to a committee, which evaluates it and assigns an official rating. This is disclosed to the issuer, who most often accepts their judgment but may occasionally appeal it for reconsideration. The rating is then released to the investing public and enters into the rater's continuing surveillance system.

Moody's (part of The Dun & Bradstreet Corporation) has been rating municipal bonds since 1918. Its public finance group is headed by Douglas Watson and currently employs about ninety analysts in New York, San Francisco, and Dallas to follow new and outstanding issues. Where do you find their ratings? In their yearly *Moody's Governments and Municipals,* a big blue three-volume set (the nearest thing to a municipal bond Bible), and also on CD-ROM. These provide a wealth of information about outstanding bond issues—financial figures, security descriptions, amounts by year, coupons, etc. Subscribers also are mailed twice-weekly loose-leaf supplement pages, with new and changed ratings. Moody's collates the original ratings and these additions and prints up a monthly red-cover book, *Moody's Bond Record.* However, these days the handiest way to find any rating is from one of the omnipresent bond screens.

Standard & Poor's (a division of the McGraw-Hill Companies) traces itself back to 1860. Its credit group covers and rates obligations of municipalities, corporations, financial institutions, insurance companies, and also structured finance securities, such as CMOs. S&P also maintains a substantial department which evaluates trust and fund portfolio bonds. In 1999 its public finance ratings section is directed by Vladimir Stadnyk, with Hy Grossman and David Goldstein heading the municipal section.

Developing from eight tax-exempt analysts in 1968, S&P's some 125 municipal analysts now follow 20,000 different bonds (including 11,000 unenhanced issues) from their New York, San Francisco, and three other offices. S&P's published ratings are updated in a number of publications, including their thick green *Municipal Ratings Handbook,* which also prints CUSIP numbers and some brief comments. In addition to their published ratings, S&P rates privately placed bonds (but does not monitor them later) and offers potential issuers confidential credit assessments of what the official letter rating will most likely be.

Fitch, established in 1913 and recapitalized in 1989, now has sixty-five analysts in New York who presently cover some five thousand tax-exempt issuers. Byron Klapper is the publisher, and Frank Rizzo is in charge of public finance, with Claire Cohen (formerly with Moody's) prominent in municipals. Fitch's tax-exempt, corporate, and other ratings, without further description, are published monthly in their gray soft-cover *Ratings Book.*

What are the differences among the three services' approaches? Each have established sets of guidelines for their ratings, not too different from our principles of bond analysis in earlier chapters. However, Moody's seems to follow the more traditional rating methodology, that is, weighting an issuer's bonded debt against its willingness and ability to pay, while S&P

usually more heavily emphasizes the economic background of the issuer. However, these two attacks seem to have blended (with Fitch somewhere in the middle), and more than 90 percent of their ratings are substantially identical. In any case, the correct way to print the three ratings is: A-1/AA-/AA, Moody/S&P/Fitch, respectively.

One point of difference. Before assigning a rating (usually triple A) to an insured bond, both Moody's and Standard rate its underlying quality. But Fitch may automatically assign its highest (AAA) rating to insured bonds, thus omitting the underlying work and charging a lower fee.

All three raters then continue to monitor the issues they have rated as long as they are outstanding. How does this surveillance work? Primarily, they check approximately one-third of all ratings annually, by reviewing financial reports from the communities. Fewer than 5 percent of these reviews result in a changed rating, recently more being raised than lowered.[1]

However, our communities sometimes surprise their bondholders unpleasantly. The raters try to anticipate or at least keep up with developments through a second process, an overview, where regional changes (such as the passage of a bond-significant referendum) and sector trends (like the deregulation of the power industry) affect the credit standing of individual municipals. When a bond's credit standing seems likely to change, the raters hoist their racing yellow flags notifying dealers and investors of a possible change.

As discussed in Chapter 4, municipalities are now required to promptly disclose *material events* affecting the credit standing of their bonds. Naturally, the agencies watch these like hawks and take appropriate action. After the situation comes into focus, the raters assign a new, definitive rating, raising the green, full-speed, flag.

In addition to ratings, the services offer a range of other municipal bond information products, as covered later in this part.

Note

1. Standard & Poor's *Public Finance Criteria,* (New York, 1997), p. 9.

20

Information Providers

During the 1990s, communications have swept over the American business scene like a series of tidal waves, with information on the financial markets, including tax-exempts, near their crest. This has led to much greater efficiency in our market and a dramatic lowering of dealer profit margins. But the new tools are indispensable, and it's impossible to survive without them. The principal broad-spectrum municipal bond information providers are McGraw-Hill, Bloomberg, Thomson, and Reuters.

McGraw-Hill

McGraw-Hill, an American company (NYSE—MHP), entered the tax-exempt information business rather quietly by buying Standard & Poor's, back when S & P was mostly a rating agency but also owned *The Blue List* (then the dominant secondary market information source). In 1990 McGraw bought J.J. Kenny, the largest tax-exempt brokerage house, along with its vast information systems. Later they acquired competing broker Clifford Drake. McGraw-Hill transmits its own products over their MuniScreen network (formerly the Kenny Drake screen). Also, over its Blue List screen it transmits hundreds of pages from most of the brokerage houses, including Kenny Drake, but not those of Chapdelaine (by direct connection only) or Cantor Fitzgerald (Reuters only). So, as of 1999, various *McGraw-Hill* divisions operate:

Standard & Poor's
Kenny Drake
K.I.S. (Kenny's bond data base)
The Blue List
The CUSIP system
A NMSIR
K-Sheets (a new issue worksheet provider)
Comstock (an extensive financial data base)

Their now approximately seven hundred subscribers (about evenly divided between dealers and others) pay by a combination of monthly and per use fees. For instance, the whole service costs about $1,700 per month per terminal.

Most particularly, McGraw can tap into Kenny Drake, their own municipal bond brokerage operation. Their most valuable information source? Kenny's nationwide bid wanted screen system. In 1999 there is also a beta version of some of their products on the Internet (www.emuni.com/disclosure.html).

Thomson

Thomson, a Canadian company (Toronto—TOC), entered the tax-exempt information market by buying the *The Bond Buyer* (continuing to publish its invaluable daily hard-copy edition), and also the then leading secondary offering service, the Munifacts wire. In 1975 they founded Securities Data Company (2 Gateway, Newark, NJ, 07102 973-622-5200). SDC provides hard copy and on-line versions of almost all competitive and negotiated new issues from 1966 on (their Municipal New Issues), in addition to Muniprofiles (17,000 municipal contact numbers and recent issue data), Municipal Market Data (yield curves and spreads), the thick red *Municipal Market Directory,* CDA/Spectrum (municipal ownership data), and a list of municipal refunding candidates (currently unrefunded, with coupons 5% or higher).

Thomson bundles most of these together, all electronically

available, in its "TM3" combined tax-exempt product. So now, these come in a single package:

The Bond Buyer
Thomson Municipal Screen
Muller (a valuation service)
CDA (a bond holdings data base)
Muniview (a municipal bond data base)
Worksheets
MMD (an analytic data base)
BidComp (a new issue bidding tool)
Dalcomp (a syndicate message network)
SDC

In addition, the *Bond Buyer* publishes an invaluable annual compendium of all sorts of tax-exempt information, its annual *Yearbook.*

Bloomberg

Privately owned, Bloomberg is now the hottest tax-exempt information provider. Everyone seems to have Bloomberg screens, and they carry almost everything anyone needs in municipals, and more. Dealers, investors, and other customers get general and financial news, municipal bond news, new issue scales, analyses, and information from a universal municipal bond description data base, along with broker pages. Bloomberg's screens are exceptionally adaptable, so you can take a dealer offering, call up that whole issue's description, get it evaluated and priced, spot it on the yield curve, and run it through a series of analytics.

Bloomberg transmits over its own screen system, and in 1999 they count over ninety thousand subscribers, several thousand devoted primarily to the municipal information. They run some other services, including bond price evaluators, who charge by the use. But Bloomberg itself has no add-on fees. However, you have to subscribe to their whole service, news, views, and all. It costs about $1,200 a month for the first terminal.

Reuters

Reuters, a British company (NYSE—RHT), transmits over its own worldwide network about 20,000 pages of its own municipal bond information and pages from 18 municipal bond brokers, including Kenny Drake and Cantor Fitzgerald. Customers pay for municipal bond news, new issue scales, analyses, and its own universal bond description data base, along with most broker pages.

Grant's

Grant's Municipal Bond Observer is a different drummer. In a nicely printed hard copy, the editor, Joe Mysak, provides personal reactions to current tax-exempt developments, along with some interesting charts. Biweekly, $625 a year, e-mail: jmysak@grantspub.com.

21

Enhancers

Insurance Companies

Back in 1987, less than 20% of the new issue volume was sold with third-party enhancement (outside guarantees). This grew to 30% in 1991 and in 1998 made up just over half. One-quarter of G.O.s and three quarters of all revenue bonds are now being sold as enhanced, mostly in the form of bond insurance.

Ambac

Each of the major bond insurers is organized as one or more operating subsidiaries of a holding company. The holding company issues stock and its own debt, and the operating company underwrites (assumes the risk of) and sells the insurance policies. So what we call Ambac (officially Ambac Assurance Co.) is the operating subsidiary of Ambac Financial Group, Inc. Ambac was the pioneer in tax-exempt bond insurance (1971). Located at One State Street Plaza, New York, it is 100 percent publicly owned (NYSE symbol ABK). With a capital of $1.4 billion, it insures the second largest amount of debt service (in 1998 over $250 billion). Ninety percent of its book is in U.S. municipals, 75% in A or better underlying ratings. S&P finds that its capital safety margin is 130–140% of expected maximum liability.[1] Note that the bonds *insured* by these companies are rated triple A. Since these obligations come before the companies' own debt, their own bonds are rated on the basis of their ability to repay investors, *not* the bonds they insure. In Ambac's case, its holding company's bonds are rated AA.

FGIC

Financial Guaranty Insurance Co. (FGIC), 335 Madison Avenue, New York, was founded in 1986. It is a subsidiary of G.E. Capital, and its capital totals over $1.5 billion. Its municipal bond insurance covers over $200 billion in debt service, mostly A or higher rated. Like the other companies, FGIC reinsures part of its risk portfolio, spreading some of the larger chunks of liability elsewhere. S&P concludes that its capital adequacy is in the 120–130% range. In 1996 it withdrew from further insuring of health care, private education, and electric utility bonds, citing their increased unpredictable risks.

FSA

Financial Security Assurance, Inc. (FSA), 350 Park Avenue, New York, started in 1986, now insures almost $100 billion in bond debt service. It is 41% publicly owned, 40% by U.S. West. Standard judges its capital along with its other payment sources, to provide a margin of safety in the 150–160% range, the highest of the major companies. However, while its insured bonds are all rated Aaa/AAA/AAA, its relatively smaller size keeps its earnings somewhat low and the market judges its insurance a hair less valuable than the others. It employs about 30 full-time municipal professionals.

MBIA

MBIA Insurance Corp. (MBIA), Armonk, New York, founded in 1986, is the largest of the bond insurers. It covers about $500 billion of debt service, with a statutory capital of $2.5 billion, and other resources of $3 billion. What other resources does MBIA, along with the other insurers draw upon to pay for defaults? Their unearned premium reserves (collected and invested, but still at risk), lines or letters of credit with other financial institutions, and stop-loss treaties. S&P figures that MBIA, in a worst-case depression background, would still be able to cover all municipal defaults, with a margin of 30 to 40% left over. In addition, should all three of their largest insured bonds (Massachusetts, Puerto Rico, and New York City) go into total immediate default, they would lose only about 25% of their capital. MBIA employs some 150 research analysts, about half conducting surveillance on its existing portfolio. MBIA's own bonds are rated AA by S&P.

How Safe Are Insured Bonds?

First, for the record, let's review the obvious: insurance is only against delay or nonpayment of principal and interest. The market price of insured bonds goes up and down, generally in the same degree as other municipals of the same maturity. But how safe actually are insured bonds? Insurers have gone so far as to say that they are safer than the best of the underlying bonds. Others think that insurance is little more than buying a triple A rating. To cover municipal bond losses, each company has its own and contingent capital sources and its reserves. To measure how these assets would cover losses involves considering: how much the company insures any one bond or class of bonds (single-risk element); future economic background (depression loss profile) and potential losses in the insurer's portfolio (capital charges); and the combined effect of these elements on the company's claims-paying ability.

The rating agencies, some dealers, and the insurers themselves have rigorously analyzed each company's claims-paying ability under a number of scenarios. Called *stress testing,* this pits the insurers' resources against their potential losses. To qualify for a triple A, the companies must solely insure securities (mono-line) and their resources must be sufficient to cover at least 125% of their estimated maximum liabilities.

The analysts' consensus opinions? (1.) That in normal times any one loss or group of losses could be readily absorbed by the insurer's resources, with business continuing as usual. (2.) That after a prolonged recession, with a moderate erosion of the market value of the insurers' own investment portfolios, the insurers would be able to meet their liabilities, dipping into capital to do so, but the insured bonds keeping their AAA ratings. (3.) That in a deep, five-or-more-year depression, with a 35% default rate, they would be almost out of capital, with only their reserves left and the insured bonds no longer AAA.

Are All Insured Bonds from the Same Company the Same?

In most markets, the biggest differences between insured bond prices in the same maturity are those of different states. The prices of all bonds, including insured paper, in such high-tax states as Connecticut, Minnesota, and Massachusetts tend to be higher than comparable bonds of states like Texas, with no or low income tax rates. However, *within* states, bonds of higher underlying ratings tend to sell at slightly lower yields than insured bonds of lower underlying quality. This is what you might expect from the consensus opinions above and may, in fact, tend to verify them.

Other Enhancers

In addition to insurance, many banks have provided letters of credit or other guarantees that issuers' financial operations will occur as promised. Has everything gone completely smoothly in this part of the enhancement business? No. Some of the guarantors, including a number of Japanese banks, have been downgraded because of their domestic troubles. But this was nothing compared to the calamitous default on their letters of credit by Mutual Benefit Life—a ten-year tangle still being unraveled. However, 99% or more of these other forms of enhancement have performed as promised.

Are All the Insurers the Same?

An American novelist—I think it was John O'Hara—back when Wall Street was an elite place, wrote that municipal bond salesmen made their living by selling fine distinctions of certainty. These days, fine distinctions may be made between the municipal bond insurers. All mono-line, all with at least an estimated 125% safety margin, all triple A. What does the market tell us? That bonds insured by Ambac, FGIC, and MBIA sell virtually identically, with FSA only a speck behind. The major companies have insured huge amounts of municipals, only a tiny percentage of which have defaulted. And all of these happily insured holders have received their principal and interest when due.

Note

1. *Standard & Poor's Bond Insurance Book* (1997) New York, p. 35 ff.

Part Six

The Investors

22

Municipal Bond Investors

So we've seen how underwriters buy new issues from communities in the primary market, how the secondary operates, and how both markets are attended by numerous service providers. Now it's time to scope the investors—those who have saved money and want to put it to work. Since 1990 investors have bought about $175 billion new issue tax-exempts per year, and still more in the secondary. How come investors buy so many? (1.) Over the years municipal issuers have repaid their bonds as promised, steadily and reliably, with very few exceptions. (2.) After personal and corporate income taxes, municipals have been providing higher returns than other fixed income securities. High in safety, superior in return—a tough combination to beat.

Safety and return are two of the three main goals for any investor—with growth of capital another. Most municipal bond investors buy tax-exempts for their safety and income and pursue growth through other investments. Who are these bond buyers? Years ago, banks, insurance companies, and individuals each bought about one-third. Since the 1970s this has changed strikingly. Now banks are buying only about 5% of the available tax-exempts, insurance companies 10%, and individuals a whopping 75%.

Reaching out for this multitude of individuals, dealers have consolidated, grown more efficient, and developed a wide range of new products. Although most dealers have had to make painful adjustments (and many quit entirely), others have grabbed the bond bull by the horns and are swinging along handsomely. This is part of the difficult but healthy restructuring of the U.S. economy a whole.

Banks

Of the three main types of U.S. banks—savings banks, savings and loans, and commercial banks—only the last are significant buyers of municipals. The others' lower tax rates usually make tax-exempts unattractive. But commercial banks pay taxes much like other corporations, with one substantial exception—they can't deduct certain municipal bond holding expenses. This reduces their tax-exempt appeal, and so banks have been buying fewer municipals recently. This exception has its own exception—bonds that are *bank-qualified.* To protect the traditional support that banks provide their own communities by investing in local issues, interest on bonds of new G.O. deals of under $10 million is exempt from this tax treatment. Therefore, *bank eligibles* currently trade about ten basis points higher than comparable bonds.

What types of tax-exempts do commercial banks favor? Usually higher grade and with shorter-than-average maturities. Whom do they buy bonds from? A mixed bag of regional and national bond dealers.

Insurance Companies

There are two main kinds of insurance companies—life, and property and casualty. Life companies, who usually pay relatively low tax rates, buy municipals sparingly. But casualty companies, who pay corporate taxes, can be substantial tax-exempt buyers, especially within one of their profit cycles. In loss years they tend to stop buying, or even liquidate, their municipals.

Most casualty companies buy in both primary and secondary markets. In search of higher yields, they often buy longer maturity bonds. Smaller ones usually buy and sell unpackaged bonds directly through regional dealers, while larger ones tend to deal with national firms. The banks and insurance companies—and also the funds and trusts—are collectively known as *institutions.*

Individual Investors

Individual people who buy securities we sometimes call *retail.* In 1998, directly or through trusts and funds, retail owned almost 75% of the outstanding municipal bonds. They amounted to some 12 million households, with average tax-exempt holdings of about $75,000. On total holdings of almost $1 trillion they received approximately $50 billion in interest and were repaid more than $75 billion in principal.

In addition to the three main groups, taxable investors, the issuers themselves, and dealers hold varying amounts of municipals.

23

Direct Investing

Unpackaged Bonds

All municipals are born in new issues, starting life as plain, unpackaged bonds. An unpackaged bond means just that—a single, freestanding municipal security, such as $100,000 principal amount of State of Alaska 5% bonds due in ten years.

Direct Investing

Most institutions and also individual investors still invest the old-fashioned direct way, by buying plain, unpackaged bonds. Sometimes from new issues, sometimes in the secondary market. Among them are some small buyers, but more independent buying traffic comes from medium- and large-sized investors. How do people go about investing in new issues? Usually when a salesman calls, pushing new issue bonds his firm is underwriting. But more likely, he will offer something from the firm's secondary trading position, as we talked about a few chapters back. Why more likely? Because getting the bonds from most new issues is an uncertain and complicated process. *And* secondary items are much more apt to carry larger commissions—which one Chicago-based salesman used to call a bond's true yield.

Buying and holding individual bonds involves some financial savvy and a number of chores, such as monitoring them for market or credit developments and checking on interest payments and redemptions, not to mention price evaluation. Institutions are well equipped to handle these duties, but many individuals prefer to finesse them, delegating them to the investment trusts and funds we cover in the next two chapters.

Short-Term Tax-Exempt Investments

We touched on municipal *notes* earlier, whereby issuers borrow for a few months to temporarily finance a local government need. These obligations (and also older tax-exempts nearing their payoff dates) are available for investors whose needs are temporary or who need *high liquidity.* Larger investors can buy these securities directly at new issue time or in the active secondary market dealers maintain in them. Smaller purchasers more often buy them through tax-exempt money market funds. Naturally, since these highly liquid short-term obligations are almost loss-proof, they usually carry correspondingly low yields.

Intermediate- and Long-Term Bonds

Investors who seek higher returns usually buy longer term holdings. For instance, when tax-exempt money markets return 3%, intermediate (five-to-fifteen-year maturity) bonds might return 5%, and long bonds (twenty-to-thirty years) might bring 6%. However, instead of being loss-free, intermediate-maturity bonds may suffer declines of up to 25% of principal in a period of sharply rising rates. And long bonds have sometimes lost 30 to 40% of principal within a few years. On the other hand, they bring in the highest yields.

Delegated Direct Investing

Although public awareness and knowledge of investing techniques have grown remarkably in the past ten years, many individuals don't have much confidence in their own financial ability. Sometimes several people are involved, complicating matters greatly, particularly when a family trust is involved. Investors in these situations may turn over the decision making to an investment manager. There are four sets of people who mind others' money—*financial planners, dealer money managers, bank trust departments,* and *regulated investment companies.*

Financial Planners

Financial planners, a relatively new breed, serve people whom Wall Street had long neglected—individuals with substantial assets and needing advice. A financial planner reviews his or her customer's life situation and offers a wide spectrum of advice ranging from tax work, through saving plans, to investment suggestions. Many are recruited from brokerage houses or through insurance companies.

The other three, dealer money managers, bank trust departments, and regulated investment companies, stick mainly to customers' investments. They go after individuals with little financial expertise but abundant assets. Some set a minimum of $500,000; others won't take anyone with less than $5 million. First they and the customer agree on an investment strategy—to put the client's money into unspecified stocks, tax-exempts, or other investments, often diversifying into several categories. Then they buy, sell, or swap holdings when the time seems right. Advertisements offering these services are generally lower-key, with pictures of little toy bulls and bears or expansive country estates, decidedly upscale, with fees to match.

Dealer Money Managers

These relatively new investment professionals usually tend portfolios of half a million dollars and up. Really dealer salespeople by another name, they naturally tend to push their firm's own products and are paid by the commissions they earn. Most of these accounts are set up as *nondiscretionary;* that is, the investor has to preapprove all transactions.

Trust Departments

The one thousand or so commercial bank *trust departments* handle about 2 million separate accounts. These accounts are typically *discretionary;* that is, they don't require specific customer trade-by-trade approval. In tax-exempts they tend to follow ultraconservative investment approaches.

Regulated Investment Companies

Regulated investment companies are licensed independent financial firms that maintain defined professional standards. They advise larger-sized individuals and institutions, mostly discretionarily. They typically charge 1% of principal annually. However, if the account is invested in 5% tax-exempts, that may come to 20% of the income, a hefty bite.

Individuals who either don't like or don't qualify for these custom services buy their tax-exempts either directly or through intermediaries—the U.I.T.s and funds we will cover later. Fortunately, we have a large variety of municipal investing choices.

24

Unit Investment Trusts

Wall Streeters had been creating stock and corporate bond packages since 1924, but they couldn't pass tax-exempt bond interest through to investors until 1961. Then Congress and the IRS relented, and Ira Haupt & Co. put together the first municipal bond bundle. Unfortunately for them, Haupt isn't enjoying their hybrid flower—the firm perished in the sordid salad oil swindle of '63.

Are we all on the same page? Let's make sure. Up to here we have tried to describe how individual, freestanding municipal bonds are created, distributed, and serviced. Now we're seeing the first way we package these bonds—into U.I.T.s. In the following chapter we cover the second way—into managed funds.

A U.I.T. is a new security that a sponsor/dealer creates by bundling together a selection of existing municipal bonds, marking up their price, and then selling to investors.

Unit Investment Trust

A fiduciary entity, closed end in structure, which holds a fixed portfolio of municipal bonds from which it distributes tax-exempt income.

The Four Trust Elements

Municipal U.I.T.s share this single form—they are *formal fiduciaries, closed end,* with a *fixed portfolio* of *tax-exempt bonds.*

1. *The trust.* Each U.I.T. is a specialized financial vehicle defined in a trust agreement between a *sponsor,* a *trustee,* and, usually, an *evaluator.* The sponsor creates and sells the U.I.T.; the trustee holds the securities, guards the rights of investors, and sends out checks; and the evaluator prices the bond portfolio. Trusts come in series under one master structure, for example, Merrill Lynch Minnesota Insured Trust. Within this series, each individual trust has its own number and CUSIP, such as Merrill Lynch Minnesota Insured Trust #23, 567890AB1. Then, when Merrill sells out #23, they package and offer #24 as quickly as they can.
2. *Closed-end.* U.I.T.s are *closed-end;* that is, shares are offered and sold to the public all at once, in a single initial public offering, or I.P.O. U.I.T. shares are called *units.* So a new $10 million trust contains 10,000 units, each with a principal value of $1,000, and the trust remains at 10,000 units until its bonds are retired. Someone buying fourteen of these units would own 14/10,000 of its worth and would collect $14,000 at maturity. And if this trust pays out 5%, or $500,000, in interest annually, the investor will also receive .14% of that, or $700 a year.
3. *Fixed portfolio and fixed maturity.* U.I.T.s are composed of unchanging portfolios of municipal securities. The sponsor typically assembles ten or more different lots of bonds and deposits (transfers ownership of) them with a trustee. The bonds remain in this particular trust permanently. No new bonds are bought and none are sold, so the original securities stay fixed and put, retaining their *original due date.* (This feature marks their chief difference from the funds.) As a result, the income U.I.T.s pay out is also fixed. A 5% trust will distribute $50 a year to each of its unit holders until the trust's

bonds are retired. Quite similar to buying a single 5% bond due in *x* years. What you see is what you get, and keep.

Tax-Exempt

Investors usually buy a trust's initial offering, hold it until maturity, and meanwhile collect interest exempt from federal and, often, state and local income taxes.

U.I.T.'s structures may seem simple, but plenty of people, even experienced salesmen, don't get it—mixing up trusts and funds. When the market was plummeting in the spring of 1987, Timmy momentarily added to the trading room's confusion by shouting out, "The trusts are selling!" Fortunately, he was quickly corrected. He meant funds, not trusts. If it has a fixed portfolio of bonds it's a U.I.T.—the only municipal bond bundle that stays permanently put, untraded, and unmanaged. (The funds, as their name says, are managed, that is, their bonds are sold and replaced as conditions change.) A package of fixed bonds? It's a trust. A package of traded bonds? It's a managed fund.

Marketing Trusts

Now a word about our sponsors, the investment houses that manufacture U.I.T.s. Some are regular dealers like PaineWebber or John Nuveen. Others are *independent investment managers,* such as Vanguard, T. Rowe Price, or Dreyfus. After a trust series structure is in place, the sponsor and/or its associated dealers form an *underwriting group* much like those for new stock or bond issues. (I've written at length on trust assembling, their prospectuses, the evaluating process, and so on, in my second bond book.[1])

Unit Pricing

When the syndicate is ready, the sponsors' trust traders buy and put aside (often in an *accumulation account*) a group of bonds meeting the trust's requirements. For long-term trusts they usually try to accumulate bonds whose price averages about 95, or $950 per unit. When they have bought enough bonds, an evaluator determines their current market price. This price may show the sponsor a profit or, rarely, a loss. Taking this evaluation, the sponsor adds on a load of about 5%, (typically bringing the retail price to near $1,000 per unit) and deposits them with the trustee. The issue then goes to the underwriters, whose sales forces offer the units to customers, at the set price. However, if the market (and the evaluated price) changes before they sell all the units, the offering price may be adjusted. If the evaluation falls 1%, then the sponsor may change the unit price by that amount, down from $1,000 to $990.

The Redemption Feature

After the issue is distributed, the units enter their own version of the secondary market. How does this operate? Unitholders can liquidate at any time, by asking the sponsors to *redeem,* that is, buy back units, at the current daily evaluation, often less a 1% charge. The sponsor may then assume the risk of reselling these old "redeemed" units to other investors, at their current evaluated price plus another load. In some markets, instead of sponsors taking on the old units, the trustee does it, by selling the underlying bonds in the open market.

Trust Portfolio Menu 1: Arranged by Credit Type

National Trusts

The first municipal bond trusts featured portfolios of long-term, medium-quality bonds in perhaps five to ten different states. For just $1,000 you could lock in a nifty 3.50%, tax-exempt, for thirty years. National trusts we call this type, and these generic U.I.T.s are still the bread and butter of every trust sponsor's restaurant. After their issuance, U.I.T. prices tend to fluctuate with the market in their underlying bonds, perhaps a bit less so because of their diversification.

State Trusts

The U.I.T. menu's special of the day is trusts with appetizing state tax exemptions—immune in some twenty-five states. Their investment characteristics are similar to those of national trusts, but they are somewhat more volatile.

Insured Trusts

In the 1970s, the municipal bond insurers began to provide coverage for entire U.I.T. portfolios, and sponsors have found that many customers will readily give up some yield for insured trusts, perhaps just 20 basis points. As with unpackaged bonds, insurance does provide protection against default, but not against losses caused by market changes.

The next step was logical—trusts that were both state-exempt and insured. For instance, in 1990 Van Kampen Merritt brought out its little $3.450 million Tennessee IM-IT Series 3 trust, all of whose bonds were covered by AMBAC and other insurance companies. Insured triple A, state-exempt, and easy to sell.

You might think that insured bonds would fluctuate less than the uninsured, but not so. Similar trusts, whether insured or not, usually go up or down together.

The Lower-Grade Trusts

Higher Yield and Lower Quality

During the early 1980s municipal bond investors got a taste of wonderfully high rates of return, 12% and sometimes more. Then, when yields fell back to more usual levels, sponsors began to tempt them with gamier trusts, composed of lower-quality, higher-yielding bonds. Most lower-grade trusts are composed of a diversified portfolio of long-term, basically sound but slightly chipped or tarnished bond situations (BBB rated, for instance). Since they are bonds that, though not gilt-edged, in all probability will pay off, their yields are usually only .50% or so higher than regular uninsured trusts. So far their volatility has roughly equaled comparable maturity national trusts, but it's hard to predict what will happen over a longer period of time.

Trust Portfolio Menu 2: Arranged by Maturity

Short-Maturity Trusts

During the 1970s U.I.T. sponsors developed trusts composed of short-, medium-, and long-maturity bonds. Short-maturity U.I.T. portfolios are normally composed of bonds due in about five years. A short trust sold in 1999 may be put together of bonds mostly due in 2004. Come 2000, its bonds will have a four-year average maturity, in 2001 three years, and will be paid off entirely by 2004, when the trust expires. Because all of the principal will be returned within a relatively short period, this kind of U.I.T. provides high price stability and low volatility. Generally speaking, if five-year maturity bond market interest rates go up 1% (as from 4.00% to 5.00%), their evaluated market worth drops only about $40, from $1,000 to $960. Combining this $40 loss with a $40 per year income, after one year a holder would be about even. (Readers may wish to contrast this with how short-term *funds* operate, in the next chapter.) Investors who hold onto short U.I.T.s get all their principal back in five years, plus the income, a sure total return. Naturally, investors pay for this low volatility. Short-term trusts will typically return around 1.5% less than long-term trusts, perhaps only about 4.00%, rather than 5.50%. Sponsors often load short-term U.I.T.s with about $20 a unit, or 40 basis points per year over a five-year life.

Intermediate Maturity Trusts

Many sponsors offer U.I.T.s with portfolios of bonds neither short nor long, the so-called *intermediate trusts.* Some are called *short intermediate trusts,* about eight years in average original maturity; they provide investors with a medium level of price stability. For every 1% that interest rates rise, these will fall in price about $60, or from $1,000 down to $940. This $60 represents more than a typical intermediate U.I.T.'s 5%, so after one year a holder would have a negative total return. Their load may average about $35, or 35 basis points over an eight-year life. Some sponsors also offer *long intermediate* trusts, whose investment characteristics fall between short intermediates and longest trusts.

Longest-Maturity Trusts

Most U.I.T. portfolios are composed of long-term bonds. In fact, when you see a trust advertised without maturity, dollars to doughnuts it's long-term. Why are they the most popular? They provide the highest returns, appealing strongly to the individual investor. Long U.I.T.s are usually invested in twenty-five-to-thirty-year bonds, exposing their holders to the greatest degree of volatility. A 1% rise in interest rates typically causes the price of a long U.I.T. to drop about 10%, or $100 per unit. This is from $1,000 down to $900, a serious fall, usually well over a year's income. Loads on longest-maturity U.I.T.s average about five points.

In the past three years a multitude of U.I.T. credit type mixtures have appeared—like the ever-new combinations in nouvelle cuisine cookery—crossbreeds of the national, state, and insured varieties. For example, intermediate-term insured Florida exempt, etc., and no doubt other kinds of U.I.T.s will be coming along soon.

Although trusts are officially formed for the benefit of their unitholders, their sponsors are the active element—first, last, and always. Sponsors accumulate bonds at their discretion and deposit them with a trustee, and its underwriting group sells them. Afterward they supervise the evaluation process, reregister the trust with the S.E.C., and (although they can't trade its bonds around) monitor the trust portfolio; if they discover serious credit troubles, they can liquidate bonds. For a nominal yearly fee, sponsors perform these and other chores until the bonds are paid off and the trust expires.

The Trust Investors

The typical U.I.T. household has one and a half incomes totaling about $75,000 per year, in 1998 held about $35,000 worth, and occasionally adds on to their holdings, rarely selling them. U.I.T.s now hold about $100 billion in municipals, 8% of all outstanding tax-exempts.

The various U.I.T. features add up to a sophisticated parcel of consumer goods—carefully shaped for high-powered advertising, and sold by persistent sales forces. U.I.T. benefits may be summarized like this:

1. *Bond selection.* Trusts are assembled by professional sponsors, so investors don't need to know a thing about the municipal bond market or its specific securities.
2. *Portfolio diversification.* Since the risk is spread among many issues, if anything happens to just one of the component bonds, investors lose only on that fraction. A

dozen eggs in twelve baskets. Protected by diversity, sponsors can securely buy medium quality and thus higher yielding, bonds.

3. *Tax-free return.* Free from federal income tax and often from state and local levies as well.
4. *Convenience.* Unitholders can lock in almost any investable amount and throw away the key, confident of receiving an income check twice a year, or even monthly. The securities are in safekeeping, are professionally evaluated, and can be redeemed at any time, producing cash within three business days.

I have referred to U.I.T.s as the lowest of the three tiers of tax-exempt investing. Among other things, they offer by far the highest tax-exempt bond commission rates. (For more on their disadvantages, see *Advisor.*) The other side of the coin is this: without U.I.T.s, many individuals wouldn't be getting tax-exempt income. You can't cover the small investor without charging a lot, and trusts certainly fit this bill. Their loads, the usual 4 to 6% markups, are fuel for the engines that propel the U.I.T. machine over difficult terrain, year after year. Naturally, the sponsors soft-pedal the load factor and dwell instead on the customer benefits. One ad showed parents smiling over their little girl tucked fast asleep in an insured U.I.T. bed. I suggest that both salespeople and customers focus on the numbers and filter out the heartwarming words.

Note

1. *The Municipal Bond Investment Advisor,* Probus Publishing Company, Chicago (1991). Copies: 212-722-8446.

25

Managed Funds

Municipal bond funds, except for what they invest in, very much resemble stock mutual funds, like the famous Fidelity Magellan, and so on. Investors started seeing them in 1976 and by 1981 were buying $4 billion worth a year. Now they are huge—close to $50 billion more was invested in them in 1998, bringing their total holdings to over $475 billion, over one-third of all outstanding tax-exempts. Managed funds provide most of the features of U.I.T.s—diversification, bond selection, tax-exempt return, and convenience. In addition, the managers trade the bonds in the portfolio. Many people, including myself, believe that tax-exempt funds represent one step up from U.I.T.s, to the second tier of municipal bond investing.

Fund investors tend to own somewhat larger and more diversified portfolios than U.I.T. buyers. About seven million households now own funds, with the average holding around $75,000. They often add on to existing or similar positions.

Tax-Exempt Open-End Mutual Fund

A *mutual* investment company whose *variable number* of shares are *priced by evaluation,* invested in an *actively managed* portfolio of *municipal securities.*

Mutual and Variable

Open-end funds are *mutual.* This means that their managers permit new investors to enter by buying, or old shareholders to exit by redeeming, their shares. Therefore, the number of shares varies, increasing or decreasing every time someone buys or sells. We saw that U.I.T.s come in handy $1,000 units, but open-end funds make it even easier to invest. They issue shares in denominations right down to thousandths. If someone likes an open-end selling for $10 and has exactly $25,500.51 in a money market account, he can switch it into 2,550.051 shares and every penny is invested.

Open-end funds are born in an I.P.O., an *initial public offering,* typically at $10 per share. Distributors may offer 25 million shares to the public, thus raising $250 million, a worthwhile amount to manage.

Priced by Evaluation

After the money is raised and invested, the fund's portfolio is evaluated daily, usually by one of the service providers, such as S&P, as mentioned. This total fund portfolio value, divided by the number of shares, produces a *net asset value* per share. So if the portfolio of the same fund is later evaluated at $225 million, the new N.A.V. would be $9 per share. All subsequent share sales, and also all redemptions, are *based* on the prevailing N.A.V. (Some distinctions follow shortly.) Many financial newspapers carry fund quotes under "Mutual Funds" headings, so you can see their current value and also the price changes from the previous day.

Managed

U.I.T.s and unpackaged bonds just sit in someone's account until they are sold or retired. Not so a mutual fund's bonds. The portfolio *changes* when new shares are bought or old ones redeemed, adjusting the size of the investment pool. In addition, managers strive to improve the investment performance of their funds, buying and selling, and also swapping, when opportunities arise. If the market is rising, their traders may sell some bonds and replace them with others they feel are more likely to go up. If, on the other hand, they believe the market is about to decline, they may reduce their more volatile holdings. In steady markets, traders try to swap from one bond into another, gaining more value. Through these and other techniques managers hope to maximize return and earn their annual management fees.

Dividends

Fund interest earnings are distributed through regular dividends, usually quarterly, safely tax-exempt by IRS ruling. However, should a fund achieve and distribute capital gains, its shareholders become liable for tax on them.

The Load Funds

Here the open-end fund road splits into two paths—load and no-load. *Load funds,* the original kind of mutual fund, are created by dealers and also by independent managers. So both Merrill Lynch and Franklin offer tax-exempt load funds. Expandable, evaluated, tax-exempt portfolio. At what price are they sold? Right at their net asset value, plus a sales fee, on long-term funds usually about 4% of principal. Their price is carried in many newspapers, both N.A.V. and also the selling price. (We cover no-loads later in the chapter.)

Dealer Load Fund Marketing

Most load funds are managed by semiautonomous corporations affiliated with general securities dealers. Funds managed by advisory companies owned by Morgan Stanley and Prudential are prominent examples. They market this product primarily through their own brokers.

Independent Load Fund Marketing

The other loaders, like Franklin, M.F.S., and Putnam, are independent distributors, not affiliated with dealers. They advertise liberally and employ their own sales forces to handle customers. In addition, some independent load funds have contracts with dealers with whom they split their fees. Merrill Lynch naturally promotes its own funds. However, they may pilot (*steer,* even) customers to Eaton Vance. Eaton Vance builds in a profit and gives up most of it to Merrill, so they—and the herd—are content.

The Redemption Price

As mentioned, load funds are sold at the N.A.V. plus a markup. What happens when a shareholder wants to sell? She can *redeem* most load funds with the manager, right at that day's closing N.A.V., *redeem* being just a fancy term for "selling." Any amount, no questions asked. In addition, a few funds charge advertising and redemption fees.

The No-Load Funds

In the 1980s a new product rose in the tax-exempt sky. Independent managers such as Fidelity, without regular brokerage customers, started offering no-load funds. No-load funds are virtually identical to load funds, except that investors may either buy or sell them right at the N.A.V. Their something-for-nothing feature gives them ammunition to compete with the traditional dealer/customer system, apparently offering the same product at a better price. How can the original load funds exist in the same investment universe as no-loads? Because they are not identical in one significant respect—service. Salespeople supply information, respond to questions, and find the best fund for their customers, and suggest switches when appropriate. It's like sitting down to a Chinese meal, where you are served, read the fortune cookie message, and walk out leaving the cleanup behind. A broker who provides such services deserves to be paid. If she doesn't, maybe a customer should dine elsewhere.

No-Load Fund Sales and Commissions

If no-loads buy or sell at the same price, how can they make money? From the fees they charge for managing the portfolio, averaging around .75% a year, 7 or 8 cents on a $10 share. This may not sound like much, but on 250 million shares it may add up to $20 million every year. What is their marketing strategy? Heavy advertising, customer response, and low-cost handling. To me, no-loads resemble a take-out-only Chinese restaurant. They advertise; you choose and pay minimally for service or atmosphere. Sometimes they'll even deliver.

The Closed-End Funds

Closed-End Fund

An investment vehicle whose portfolio is *actively managed,* and whose *fixed number* of shares are *priced by market action.*

Closed-end funds, like the mutuals, are new (derivative) securities, created by a manager, who actively manages the fund's portfolio. They differ from the more common mutuals in two main respects—the number of their shares stays constant, rather than changing every day, and their shares trade on a stock exchange according to current supply and demand, rather than by evaluation. Most closed-ends trade on the New York Stock Exchange, where investors pay a commission as on any regular stock transaction. The first closed-end, Granddaddy Nuveen—came out in 1988, and almost every month we now see a new closed-end I.P.O.

So nobody gets lost here, remember that all funds, open- and closed-end, are managed. On a continuum between the 0% no-loads and the 4% loads, closed-end funds represent a midway point, since exchange commissions average 1 or 2% on small orders. Some dealers, especially discount brokers, have blurred this nice distinction, offering a broad spectrum of tax-exempt funds, high-, medium-, low-, and no-load.

Except for the way they're priced, closed-end funds act much like open-ends in the marketplace, and now we'll treat them similarly.

The Fund Portfolio Menu 1: Arranged by Credit Type

National Funds

The first municipal bond funds, the generic, no frills line, were composed of portfolios of investment grade, nationally diversified bonds. We call them *national funds,* and they are still the largest selling single variety, with about a 30% market share. Their portfolios are composed mainly of average to good quality bonds. National funds limit credit risk by diversifying, spreading their investment over many different bond issues, both as to location and as to credit types. For example, in the original $598 million Shearson Managed Municipals portfolio, the largest single holding within any state was $49 million of various bonds within Texas, or only 8% of the total. Funds also watch out for overconcentration on one security type, usually avoiding owning too many housing or health care bonds, for example.

State Funds

With state and local taxes sometimes running more than 10% on out-of-state municipal bond interest, investors have long been buying unpackaged blocks of instate tax-exempt bonds. The funds now compete—about 40% of them are now single-state exempt. What yields do state funds carry? Usually something like 25 basis points lower than national funds. In 1998, when the largest national funds were offered at 5.00%, ten New York-exempt funds carried only about an average 4.75%. After New York's 35-basis-point bite on other states' bonds, investors came out ahead.

The Insured Funds

Although more than 99% of all tax-exempts issued in recent years have met their obligations in full and on time, a few have not. During less stable economic cycles, notably during the early 1930s, a sizable number of issuers defaulted. In addition, the various urban bond crises of 1974–76 still echo, if faintly. As covered, a number of powerful insurance companies sell policies against default, and funds investing only in these began to appear in the early 1980s. Their triple-A bond ratings have made a great impression on investors, and in 1998 the bonds in about half of all funds were so protected. In most markets, they offer about 20 basis points less than comparable uninsured funds. That's the price investors pay for antidefault pills. Fund ads correctly point out that it's the portfolio that's insured and not the shareholders' market value.

Lower-Grade Funds

The wonderfully fat interest rates of the early eighties lured a great number of individual investors into our markets. Some fund operators, calling themselves high-yield, aggressive, or high-income, have tried to recapture some of those returns by putting together funds of higher-yielding, but lower-grade, municipal bonds. They have grown at an annual rate of 17%, and now they comprise 7% of all tax-exempt funds. We sometimes call them "junk" funds, but not to their faces, and in fact, this highly charged word doesn't entirely fit them. Many of their managers assemble maximum return portfolios through two devices—by buying premium bonds and buying bonds just below standard investment quality.

The Fund Hybrids

What happens if a customer's investment requirements are both short and insured, or New York and intermediate maturity? No problem; he just orders up one of the new hybrids, a New York Intermediate Insured.

The Fund Portfolio Menu 2: Arranged by Maturity

Funds Live Forever

Whether open- or closed-end, most fund families offer a variety of portfolio *maturity* types, from very short-term money market to those with longest due dates. As detailed, the maturity of U.I.T.s and unbundled bonds grows shorter with the passage of time. But not so with managed funds. Their portfolios remain a constant five, ten, or thirty-five years out. Why? Because as time passes, fund managers sell or swap the shortened maturities and replace them with longer ones, rarely allowing them to mature. Therefore, *the market value of managed funds, even shorter-term ones, does not necessarily return to 100 cents on the dollar at any specific time.* If an investor pays $8 a share for a fund originally issued at $10, its value may never return to $10. Indeed, many a fund started when rates were lower sat at $7 or $8, even after a prolonged period of falling rates. Why do the managers regularly lengthen their portfolio maturities? To reach for higher yields and to keep the fund, and its management fees, alive.

Back to the Yield Curve

We talked about the yield curve and saw how shorter maturity dates mean lower volatility and longer ones higher. In the U.S. economy, demand for short-dated, *highly liquid, low-volatility* investments is usually greater than for long ones, resulting in *higher* prices and therefore lower interest rates. Don't you sometimes *have* to settle for any available interest rate in order to have quick, 100 cents on the dollar, access to your money? Now let's see how the yield curve applies to funds, short, intermediate, and out long.

The Money Market Funds

Tax-exempt money market funds first appeared in 1980. They are mutual, open-end, and no-load. Everybody seems to be running one these days. Independents such as Scudder, Stevens and Clark, and also dealers, for instance Tucker, Anthony, who keep part odd bits of my money busy between other investments. Money market funds are priced at $1 each and are designed to stay right there. Buy at $1, sell at $1, no fluctuations, and no load. (Naturally, like no-load funds, they make their money taking part of the portfolio's income.) In return for maximum liquidity investors accept whatever short-term yields are available.

This breed of fund invests in municipal notes and other obligations that come due within a few weeks or months, thus avoiding fluctuations from their one-dollar value. Some stay ultra-liquid, owning only high-grade, shortest-term securities, while others may go out a little longer. In early 1998, individuals could get a 3.50% tax-exempt, a little better than a taxable money market rate of 4.75%, which was providing about a 3.25% after tax.

Short Funds

Moving on from virtually risk-free parking places to permanent investing in tax-exempts, we go out a few years on the yield curve. The tax-exempt money market funds provide *maximum liquidity;* the long-term funds offer *maximum income.* In between lie the *short-* and *intermediate*-maturity funds, which offer moderate liquidity and moderate income. *Short* funds, such as U.S.A.A.s, emphasize the liquidity aspect by investing in portfolios due in about five years. If interest rates rise by 1% for five consecutive years, you can expect that short managed funds will lose about 20% of their principal value.

Intermediate Funds

Intermediate funds, such as Vanguard's Municipal Intermediate, emphasize the income aspect more strongly. They typically invest in bonds due in ten to fifteen years. Five years of rising interest rates will probably bring a loss of about 30% to a fifteen-year maturity fund. In the fall of 1998 intermediate-term national funds were paying about 4.00%.

In addition, a few shorter funds take a different approach, limiting their purchases to an exact maturity. Their bonds are traded around some but will all gradually come due, thus acting almost like unpackaged bonds due in that year.

Long-Maturity Funds

The most common maturity fund type is composed of bonds due from twenty-five to forty years out. This is natural, since the majority of tax-exempt holders are in for the long haul, where the highest yields are usually found. The safety of principal ranges from high to extremely high. But the market prices of long term bond funds depend on the level of competing interest rates. The N.A.V. of long funds will probably decline by about 35 to 40 percent in a five-year period of sharply rising rates. Long term funds were returning about 5.00% in late 1998.

The Open-End Fund Prospectus

Mutual fund prospectuses similar to new issue O.S.s, come in many sizes and formats. They are often written in two parts, called A and B, uninspiredly. The first pages of part A usually list: some *essential financial information;* a statement of the fund's *investment objectives;* a part dealing with various *options* offered to shareholders; and, finally, a *general information* section. *Part B* (or a *Statement of Additional Information*), usually appearing in a separate folder, contains the technical details, and describes the fund's latest portfolio. No matter how large a fund grows to be, all of its shares are issued under just one prospectus, amended periodically.

Part A

On page 3 of most prospectuses the fund is defined as an *open end investment company*—that is, owned by its shareholders. If the fund is national, the word *diversified* is added, meaning that its portfolio consists of a wide variety of securities; if the portfolio is narrowly composed, such as all Ohio-exempt and insured, it's *non-diversified.* The legal jurisdiction under whose laws the fund operates, the date of incorporation, and the par value of the shares (a purely technical item) are often mentioned here. Then comes the fund's *strategy,* or its investment aim. This is often vaguely worded, such as "To provide as high a level of interest income exempt from Federal taxes, as is consistent with prudent investing, while seeking preservation of shareholders' capital." Next comes a brief summary of the fund's *bond portfolio character,* such as: "The Fund will seek to achieve this objective by investing primarily in long-term, high- and upper-medium quality municipal bonds." Often the lawyers insist on sticking in some emergency provisions—the fund's right to buy taxable obligations (though no tax-exempt fund I've ever seen has), etc. If a fund is limited to bonds of a specified credit quality it says so here.

Fund Yield

Where in the prospectus do you find the fund yield? Nowhere. They don't project their future returns at all. Who knows what a fund or its traders will do next? Besides, the SEC won't allow it. So, they just report past returns, calculating the yield of every bond in the portfolio for the last thirty days and also the last year. (The thirty-day yield is a tolerable substitute for current yield, excluding any load.)

If someone invests $100,000 in a 5% unpackaged bond due in fifteen years, he can expect a regular $5,000 annual return. But if a fund has returned 5% in the past 30 days and the past year, you can't be sure about what it will return in the future. Managers can't and don't guarantee the level of future dividends. In fact, they specifically state that past income is no guide to future results. As managers switch portfolios around, the principal amount, interest income, and also maturity length of their bonds stay in flux. This provides their appeal to some investors—their money is being managed. For other people, that's a drawback, since fund income and risk levels are hard to predict.

Services and Warnings

Buried in most fund, and also unpackaged bond and U.I.T. prospectuses, under "Municipal Securities" or "Special Consideration," come warnings about the horrendous risks of owning municipals. Here surfaces one kind of Wall Street schizophrenia. Fund ads paint a cheerful, yield-full picture, while their prospectuses harp on catastrophes. New York State funds make particularly frightful reading. I can picture the lawyers fretting—maybe they'd left out something awful. So they add:

"There are, of course, numerous variations in the security of municipal bonds (general obligation, revenue, and other), within particular classifications and between classifications, depending on multiple factors." What is the effect of these disclaimers? To make the prospectus so unrealistically alarming that the buyers return to the ads.

The same approach holds for the witless warnings about changes in interest rates. "The market values of municipal bonds may in certain circumstances decline in response to rising interest rates" gives you the idea. Just look at the figures, so you can steer a middle course.

Two or more divisions of a single distributor may be employed to handle different aspects of a fund's business. So, parent Merrill Lynch and Company, Inc., has a subsidiary, Merrill Lynch Asset Management (MLAM), which in turn has a subsidiary, Fund Asset Management, Inc. (FAMI), which manages their large California Municipal Bond Fund (Calamity?), among many others. Still another division may perform the clerical work, all billings included in the expense figures.

Part B

Late in Part B appears a list of the bonds in the latest available portfolio. These are usually arranged by state, with percentages of various kinds, to give an idea about the bond diversification. Naturally the managers shift their bonds around fairly often, so this list gives only a general idea about the holdings. Also, a list of the fund's underwriters appears, along with their share of the offering.

So that finishes our packaged bond section: U.I.T.s with fixed portfolios and fixed maturities; funds, both open- and closed-end, with managed portfolios and lengthening maturities—both kinds offering many types of bonds to choose from—and, with no doubt, more kinds coming.

Part Seven

The Regulators

26

Regulation

Securities Exchange Commission

The SEC was created by the Securities Exchange Act of 1934, as the New Dealers set about fixing the 1920s' financial market wreck. Its aim? To promote fair and efficient stock and bond market dealing. The first Commissioner, Joseph P. Kennedy, was appointed by F. D. Roosevelt, who supposedly remarked, "Set a thief to catch a thief." Congress has amended the Act many times, and the Commission itself frequently reinterprets it. What about our favorite subject, tax-exempts? The Act originally exempted both municipal and Treasury dealers because the general public bought so few bonds from them, with abuses occurring rarely.

Joe Kennedy was followed by many distinguished and other commissioners. In 1999, we have Arthur Levitt, formerly of CBWL, who has staked out his own high ground, riling many dealers and forcing the NASD to knuckle under. My own reactions to him? Natural resentment toward regulators, plus grudging admiration.

NASD

SEC legislation of 1933 and 1934 created a place for self-regulatory organizations (SROs) such as the New York Stock Exchange. In 1938 the Maloney Act Amendments authorized the National Association of Securities Dealers (NASD) to help Congress write workable securities rules. These defined proper practices, prohibited fraudulent and dangerous activities, and provided mechanisms to detect and punish the thieves. However, through the late 1960s, the markets were chiefly regulated by the SEC. Then the great paperwork crisis hit Wall Street, and the SROs came to life. Both the SEC and the SROs regulated dealers until the early 1980s, when Congress eliminated direct SEC market supervision.

So two sets of regulators now oversee Wall Street—the federal government's SEC, the writer and approver of rules, and the SROs, their enforcers. Overt cooperation between public and private sectors. Over the years this self-regulatory mechanism has been much modified and added to, and has proven greatly successful.

Municipal Bond Regulation

For forty-two years municipal bond dealers remained exempt from the SEC Act. But by the 1970s two things had happened:

1. *Individuals.* As discussed in earlier chapters, individual investors came pouring into municipals in the 1960s. Tax-exempt funds hadn't appeared yet, and many bond firms sprang up, particularly in California, Florida, New Jersey, and New York. They had a new market waiting for them, free from two regulatory burdens—the paperwork, and capital requirements. Most of these new dealers behaved fairly and ethically. But Washington became uneasy, as the general public played a larger and larger role in this unregulated part of the securities market.
2. *Memphis.* Back in 1960, about 18,000 commercial banks were operating in the United States, most of them small and relatively unsophisticated. And Memphis was perhaps the country's number-twenty bond town, with five dealers and a couple of dealer banks. Then two men there, Mr. M. and Mr. L., began to see things differently.

Banks were their game. Dozens of dealers began operating in Memphis and in Little Rock, with many, such as Mr. M., conducting bank business fairly. Then the number of dealers burgeoned there—dividing like amoebas until there were almost 100 of them! With names such as Federal Reserve Securities, Inc. Imagine, "Mr. Bank President, this is Federal Reserve calling!" Suddenly Memphis was our second municipal bond city, trading in unheard-of volume. Their favorite technique? Say a little Illinois bank was suffering with a block of then short-term 1 1/2% bonds bought at 100 back in the low interest rate 1950s. In 1965 they were worth 80. Selling them at that price would reduce the bank's capital, pinching their lending business. But here was a Memphis salesman not only offering to pay him his cost, 100, but also sell him good quality long-term 4% municipals at the same price, 100—even-Steven! The gimmick? The long 4s were worth only 75.

Well, of course all bubbles finally burst, this one popped by the Comptroller of the Currency. He changed Regulation T, telling banks to stop making adjusted tax-exempt trades, period. The Memphis Bond Daddies fled, closing firms by the dozens. But reputable firms there continued, business as usual. A fine bond reunion was held there in the summer of 1998, to revisit the old days and ways. And Mr. L.? Shot dead many years ago by parties unknown.

The MSRB

In the early '70s, with the public buying heavily, abuses spreading, and Congress, led by Sen. Harrison A.(Pete) Williams of New Jersey, on the warpath, we got word that regulation was inevitable. Our industry representatives spent many months in Washington helping to hammer out new dealer rules. Beginning in 1975, all municipal dealers were required to join the NASD and became subject to the standards of a new self-regulatory organization, the Municipal Securities Rulemaking Board (MSRB).

Like many organizations, the MSRB is composed of a board and a staff. Its fifteen-person board is composed of representatives from five dealers, five dealer banks, and five nonindustry parties (including one issuer and one investor). And also a full-time Washington-based staff. Who pays for the NASD and the MSRB? Dealers do, through assessments on transactions. How about Treasury dealers? They remain officially, but lightly regulated by the NASD.

MSRB regs come in three sections: Administrative Rules, Definitional Rules, and General Rules. Copies of the regulations, revised annually, may be seen in any dealer comptroller's or lawyer's office.

From day to day what does the MSRB do?

1. Acts as a buffer between dealers and the SEC.
2. Writes rules governing dealer behavior.
3. Issues rulings on municipal matters, both upon theoretical request and in disputes.
4. Maintains an extensive data bank of official statements, and consultant and political contributions.
5. Issues daily tax-exempt trading reports.

The MSRB, headed effectively for many years by Christopher (Kit) Taylor, is located at located at 1150 18th Street, N.W., Washington, DC 20036 (202-223-9347). If you have an out-of-the-ordinary question about municipals, you can expect a courteous and helpful response from its staff members.

Who really regulates Wall Street? We do. Including you, my readers, now or in the future. I look at it this way. Who keeps you from stealing easy money or beating up some ninety-pound weakling? You do. Of course there are laws against such behavior, police to enforce those laws, and judges and juries to punish infractors. But day in, day out, although our SROs keep many employees busy, require tons of paperwork from dealers, and often issue dramatic statements, the market's professional participants set its own standards. I know of no business that has any higher. The simplest ways to express bond ethics? "Don't lie; don't cheat; don't steal."

27

Arbitration

Differences

On an average day for every million transactions that take place in the U.S. securities markets, around 995,000 go through without trouble. But on the remaining 5,000 or so the parties disagree with the terms of the trade—usually about price or description. Most of these we call *differences,* that is, misunderstandings, unintended errors, or the like. A ticket for 1,000 shares was written up as 100 shares, or the actual price of 78 was typed as 87. Most of these are soon corrected. But perhaps 500 remain unresolved, such as problems with limit stock orders: "I told you to sell Compaq at 35 or higher, and you sold it at 34 3/4." "No, you didn't." This kind of dispute brings negotiations directly between the parties—either a customer and a dealer or two dealers. Most of these are settled, often through compromise.

Problem Trades

Fifty or so problem trades remain, involving more controversial matters. Were the securities represented correctly? Were they suitable for that customer? Were they traded in and out too quickly? When these issues surface, dealer branch managers typically intervene and explain and settle about half of them. Sometimes they make an adjustment, by canceling one or more trades. The branch managers fail to settle about twenty-five cases. Enter the dealer's compliance officers, who iron out many of those remaining. That's one of their jobs.

The most difficult cases—which may surface months or years after the original transactions—at first proceed through the same path. Salesman, branch manager, compliance. If the parties can't agree, lawyers for both sides usually enter the picture. Often one or both sides see the light and either the dispute is dropped or a compromise is made. Nationwide, about 7,000 cases a year remain unresolved, and one of the parties calls for arbitration. Of these relatively few involve municipals.

The Predispute Clause

Why arbitration? Why not the court system? Because most dealers, wary of unpredictable and extravagant jury awards, and legal costs, now only accept customers who sign a predispute arbitration clause in their new account contract. Look at one and you'll surely see the clause, often in capital letters.

The New York, American, and local stock exchanges, the NASD, and the commodities and options exchanges all operate their own arbitration systems. Each conforms to the design of SICA, the industrywide arbitration organization. The MSRB now sends its cases to other SROs, principally the NASD.

An Alternative to the Court System

Basically, arbitration is a civil minicourt, connected to the regular judicial system but operating parallel to it. It has been tested and approved at all governmental levels. Arbitration awards are appealable to the courts, but only under extremely limited conditions. Almost all appeals are turned down. Arbitration rulings are meant to stand, except in gross miscarriages of justice. And they usually do.

How does the securities arbitration system work? There's a regular routine. The initiating party (called the *claimant*) files a Statement of Claim with the SRO, alleging damages, and the other side (the *respondent*) answers it. Then the SRO's arbitration department creates a panel of experts to manage, hear, and decide each case. Sometimes the parties, seeing each other's positions detailed in writing, come to a settlement. If not, the case proceeds to *discovery,* the process whereby the parties exchange information and documents. Within a few months, the arbitrators set a time and place for the hearing, generally near the locale of the claimant.[1]

The Hearing

The panel is usually composed of three arbitrators, two from outside the industry, one serving as chairman. In practice, one arbitrator will be a lawyer and another one familiar with the field in dispute. As in court trials, at the *hearing,* first come summaries of the case by attorneys from both sides. Then the claimant's lawyer calls one or more witnesses, sees them sworn in, and examines—that is, questions—them, subject to objections by the other side and rulings by the panel. Then the respondent's lawyer cross-examines. Next one or more witnesses from the respondent's side take the stand, are questioned by their lawyer, and are cross-examined. This ends the fact witness part of the hearing. Fact witnesses are supposed to stick to what actually happened and refrain from expressing opinions.

Experts

Now come the *expert witnesses,* sometimes several for both sides. First come questions to the experts hired by the claimants, then cross, then questions to the respondent's experts, followed by cross. What is an expert—a hired gun or a well-credentialed supplier of opinions? In my experience, experts for the weaker side usually seem specious and hired. Opposing lawyers love them, sometimes grilling them unmercifully or, after amply demonstrating their weakness, dismissing them, seemingly generous. Experts for the stronger side often seem more informed and objective. The opposing lawyers either try to break them or to get them off the stand as soon as possible.

How long do hearings take? Usually from one to three days. But I saw one where the weaker side dragged it out for fifteen. They paid, heavily.

After the witnesses are finished, the lawyers sum up, and the hearing is over. The arbitrators consult and render an award within thirty days. These awards are usually made without explanation, just the dollar amounts. Dealers have to pay, period. As noted, almost all awards stand.

The Fairness Issue

If a typical court case takes three years, SRO cases last about ten months and cost each side 50 percent less. How fair to customers are SRO arbitrations? In 1991 the General Accounting Office studied the issue. They found that compared to other arbitration forums, such as the American Arbitration Association, SROs were slightly more generous to public customers. Two other GAO findings: (1.) Customers who acted as their own counsel get about 40% lower awards. (2.) The arbitrators were undertrained. In response, the SROs now mandate thorough arbitration prep courses.

In my experience the arbs bend over backward to act and decide equitably, especially with individual claimants and most particularly with the more unsophisticated, no matter how personably objectionable. Expert witnessing is my third career in municipals. Trading, writing, witnessing—in my father's house there are many mansions.

All in all, I see arbitration as an admirable system. But I'd like to suggest one improvement. I've run into too many cases where dealers haven't paid up, to both customers and other dealers. They transfer assets or plead inability to pay. It's not right to allow them to continue, possibly bilking more people. Why doesn't SIPC insure payment of all awards? Its function is to protect people from dealer malfeasance, and they certainly are cash-heavy, recently reducing fees because their claims are so light. And why not raise SIPC's out-of-date regular coverage limits? $500,000 isn't what it used to be.

Note

1. For a detailed description of the arbitration process, see David E. Robbins's *Securities Arbitration Procedure Manual* (Third edition, 1998. Lexis Law Publishing).

Index